T0354608

IN THE FRIGHTENED HEART OF ME

TENNESSEE WILLIAMS'S LAST YEAR

TONY NARDUCCI

IN THE FRIGHTENED HEART OF ME
TENNESSEE WILLIAMS'S LAST YEAR

iUniverse books may be ordered through booksellers or by contacting:

iUniverse
1663 Liberty Drive
Bloomington, IN 47403
www.iuniverse.com
1-800-Authors (1-800-288-4677)

ISBN: 978-1-4759-6594-0 (sc)
ISBN: 978-1-4759-6595-7 (hc)
ISBN: 978-1-4759-6596-4 (e)

Library of Congress Control Number: 2013900776

Print information available on the last page.

iUniverse rev. date: 12/01/2016

CONTENTS

CHAPTER 1

SAILOR TENNESSEE WILLIAMS

KEY WEST, FLORIDA: FEBRUARY 1982

"Would you like a kind stranger to help?" I asked, unrehearsed, tongue in cheek, wondering if anyone used that line before when meeting him for the first time. However, since he was stumbling down the stairs and in need of help, it made perfect sense. What I didn't know was how ominous Blanche's words would be.

He turned from the railing he'd clutched with both hands, looked at me wide-eyed over thick, TV-screen glasses, and, without acknowledging my clever introduction, he returned the courtesy. "Yes, I believe I could use some help."

It was Tennessee Williams.

Suddenly, I was cast in the role of the good doctor in *A Streetcar Named Desire;* he was Blanche Dubois, vulnerable and needing the kindness of a stranger. Like the doctor who rescued Blanche from oblivion, I would rescue him from despair, at least for a moment. I held his left arm with my left hand and wrapped my right arm around his shoulder. Slowly, we descended the stairs of the Monster—the outdoor disco that was the nightly haunt of men on the prowl.

Tennessee Williams, the most accomplished modern playwright and perhaps one of the greatest artists of the twentieth century. His plays were renowned throughout the world. Many of them had been made into films: *The Glass Menagerie*; *A Streetcar Named Desire*; *Cat on a Hot Tin Roof*; *Sweet Bird of Youth*; *Suddenly, Last Summer*, and *Night of the Iguana*. Hollywood's best, brightest, and most famous brought his resonant characters to the stage and screen.

Icon of the 1950s, sought-after guest on TV talk shows, newsmaker famous for scandalous behavior, champion of sexual liberation, openly gay man, father of some of the best plays ever written. I watched him interviewed on talk shows, followed his career, saw all his plays. I read everything by him or about him. He was instantly recognizable to me. He was my hero.

This was the genius who redefined theater by stripping away old-fashioned, extraneous conventions. His plays read like modern poetry. I was fourteen when I first fell in love with his work. He taught me about life. He was my Socrates, my Wizard of Oz. He inspired me to be an artist. I knew him well, but I didn't know him at all.

Now I was seeing him up close. He looked old, tired, a

Kabuki version of himself. Gnarled strands of dry, white hair wrapped his head like an unraveling bandage and owl eyes, magnified by his glasses, looked frightened.

Just a kid then, I wanted him to probe my soul, resolve the dilemma of what to do with my life. I was certain he had the answers. Here I was, rescuing my hero from plummeting down a flight of stairs. It was the beginning of the most significant redefining moment of my life, and the end of his most illustrious career in American theater.

In the late 1970s and 1980s, Key West was a popular destination for many gay men escaping the cold northern winter. The tiny key had everything a gay man wanted: endless sunshine, beaches, bars, and easy, abundant sex. It was the time before the world fought HIV/AIDS infection, when gay men were unworried and promiscuous, and this place was paradise.

I made my first visit in 1979. My friend Albert moved to the tiny coral reef in the late 1970s. He was one of the early gay pioneers who came to resurrect the island from the quiet, shabby town it had become into the rollicking gay resort it would be. It was gay Mecca in those days, and I loved to make the pilgrimage.

From early childhood, I was creative and independent, confident I would do something artistic with my life. I had been making films for three years, but I wasn't making money and had many bills to pay, so I accepted a job working for Xerox as a sales trainer, at first part-time and then a year later as a full-time employee, and I hated it. The business world was filled with insincere, opportunistic, boring people. Compared to film, the work was meaningless. I desperately wanted to return to filmmaking, but I was in my early thirties, indigent, and knew the time had come to be responsible and have a career. The "starving artist" thing wasn't working for me; however, the corporate world was alien to me. I needed something to "jump-start" the dormant artist.

I came to Key West to reflect on my life. How did I get here? What should I do? I was passionate about filmmaking, and I was good at it! So why wasn't I making money? At that point, it had been almost two years since I'd entered the business world. I was looking for the thread to pull me back to the film world I loved. Maybe I was kidding myself, but it was now or never to decide which path I would take: business or film.

That was the fourth February in a row that I'd made the journey to this island of earthly delights. Each year, a posse of gay men from Chicago would arrive the last week in February and stay at the Lighthouse Court. It was a gay compound—an all-day party that lasted all week.

This gay playground got its name from the ancient lighthouse next door that rose like a giant phallus, marking the spot where the boys were. In the eighteenth and nineteenth centuries, the beacon guided sailors into shore; now, it was still guiding marauding men to its shores.

Pirates were among the first sailors. After plundering ships, they would voyage to Key West to bury their treasure, relax in the sun, and prepare for the next plunder. Pirates and sailors symbolized the ultimate gay fantasy—hundreds of young, half-naked, tightly clad renegade men traveling aimlessly for days on a ship full of other men. That lifestyle represented freedom, sex, adventure, openness, and debauchery. This history gave a gay romantic quality to this pile of white coral, set at the southernmost point in the United States, somewhere between the Atlantic Ocean and the Gulf of Mexico.

Across the street from the compound was the house where Ernest Hemingway lived during the 1940s and where he wrote some of his best work: *A Farewell to Arms* and *For Whom the Bell Tolls.*

His favorite hobbies were fishing, carousing, and, of course, plenty of drinking. Hemingway's stories read like the gay lifestyle as well, adventurous men who are either impotent, in flight, or in peril, and therefore unable to settle down with a woman, yet always ready for an affair or a fling. This isn't far off from how many gay men live.

Some critics believe Hemingway was a closet homosexual and may have had an affair with F. Scott Fitzgerald. Gay men love to believe all this folklore because it adds to the romantic allure of the island.

Mornings at the Lighthouse Court would begin with classical music and a light poolside breakfast of fresh-squeezed orange juice, coffee, and a croissant. Coffee was the hangover remedy for the night before, and the energy booster to start the new day's adventures. After lying in the sun for two or three hours, we'd be ready for a walk down Duval Street for lunch, shopping, and cruising for "fresh meat." Then we'd head back to the guesthouse for a dip in the pool, a nap, or for some late-afternoon sex. Each day was the same, but each felt like a new adventure.

Evenings would begin with a frenzy of outfit changes, looking for the perfect combination of shirt and jeans to allure a trick for the night. All the fussing was more fun than necessary. Ultimately, we would take off our shirts and dance wildly through the night at the Monster. Sharing the experience made for rich gossip the next day.

Tonight, however, instead of hanging with our posse, I was having dinner with my best friend, John Kauppilla.

The night was magical. Cobalt twilight, an oceanside table, a bottle of wine, and soul-searching conversation set the stage for a great dinner and a great adventure. This would be the night I would meet my literary hero, Tennessee Williams.

After a fabulous seafood dinner and our usual finale of cognacs, we headed off to dance. The sapphire sky had turned blue-black. The stars were points of white light, like diamonds in a queen's gown, dazzling as she walked across the sky. The air was sweet with the scent of flowers. Tiny magenta bougainvillea bells jingled in the wind.

We entered the Monster to the familiar pulsating sound of loud disco music and a crowd of sweaty bare-chested men. The Monster was completely outdoors, with cantilevered decks suspended over a wide-open atrium dance floor. I told John to wait downstairs by the dance floor, while I scurried upstairs to the less crowded bar to get us two more cognacs.

I'd leapt up the first flight of stairs and turned to leap up the second, when suddenly I halted in midflight. There was Tennessee Williams, slowly beginning his descent down the two flights of precarious stairs. He looked dressed for a costume party. Wearing a white cotton sailor suit with a matching white captain's cap, the bottoms of his trousers rolled, he looked comical. I noticed he was barefoot and struggling to get down the crowded stairs. As he was about to tumble, I reached to stop him from falling.

"Would you like a kind stranger to help?" I asked. This was more than a coincidence—it was destiny!

Exactly a year ago on this same flight of stairs, I'd watched him ascend. That night he'd worn a black dock worker's hat and a multicolored fur coat. I'd thought that odd, as it was 72 degrees. He looked half thug, half drag queen that night. Seeing him now, dressed as a sailor, made me think he might wear costumes to "try on" characters for his plays.

That first night a year ago, a bevy of young men buzzed around him, basking in the glow of the great playwright's fame. I stepped toward him but stopped, unsure of what to say. I didn't want to be an intrusive fan or, worse yet, a sycophant like the others. I watched as the opportunity to meet him slipped away. I regretted not being more assertive.

However, tonight was different. He was stumbling down the stairs, alone and needing help. It was an honest way of meeting him. We teetered down the two flights of stairs to the men's room. When we arrived, he turned and looked at me intently.

"Would you mind waiting to escort me back up those challenging stairs?"

"I'd love to!" I replied as he walked into the restroom. I was tingling. How could I continue to engage him? What would we talk about? Fawning is not in my DNA. The narrow bathroom hallway, laced with men in shadow, smelled of urine. Thelma Houston's "Don't Leave Me This Way" blasted through the space. He returned, smiling.

"You look familiar. Have we met before?" Could he have noticed me a year ago, or was this how sailors met? The familiar scent of fresh meat, the rush of lust, and a yearning desire to make contact made everyone look familiar.

"I saw you a year ago in this same place on these same stairs. You were with a lot of people."

"Perhaps I did notice you!" he exclaimed. I wasn't sure what to say next, so I smiled. "Do you mind if I hold on to your shoulder?" he flirtatiously asked.

"Please do," I enthusiastically replied. He put his right

hand on my shoulder and used the other to clutch the stair rail. This was what I'd hoped for, ever since I first came to Key West—an adventure with Tennessee Williams. As we began to scale the stairs, he turned to look at me with a big painted smile smeared across his face. He was wearing makeup. A glint of light in his glasses twinkled at me. With his gaze fixed on me, I felt I could fly.

"Could I return the kindness by buying you a drink?"

I was struck by his gentility. "Thank you."

"What would you like?" he graciously asked.

We sat at a table full of young men. A flood of recollections came to mind. *The Glass Menagerie*, high school English, sophomore year:

"Why does Laura collect glass objects?" Miss Scott asked. Eagerly, I raised my hand, and she nodded at me.

"She's shy and uncomfortable around people. She prefers to escape into a world of her own imagination. The glass menagerie is her refuge."

"Good answer."

The Glass Menagerie, American theater course, college sophomore:

Dr. Herbert asked, "What is the significance of the glass unicorn?" I eagerly raised my hand. "Yes?"

"Laura is like the unicorn, fragile and unique. When the gentleman caller drops it and the horn breaks off, it symbolizes that he has helped Laura feel normal ... accepted."

"Good."

The Glass Menagerie, freshman honors literature class, as a first-year English teacher:

"Why does Laura collect glass objects?" I asked the class.

With that prelude flashing in my mind, I wanted to ask him a million questions. How much of Laura was based on his sister, Rose? Was his mother really like Amanda in the play? How do I become an artist? What should I do with my life?

"Cognac," I said to Tennessee.

"Sebastian, would you mind?" A tall blond Viking of a young man scurried off to get the elixir. The night was hot, the air rife with testosterone. Bare-chested men continually cruised the area around our table. The place was full of hungry predators. I wanted Tennessee all to myself. How could I have a conversation when all these sycophants were staring at me? But Tennessee was focused on me.

"Where are you staying?" he asked.

"The Lighthouse Court."

"Is it very nice?"

"Oh yes, it's great! Charming rooms, a swimming pool, and a small patio for breakfast and lunch make it a pleasure oasis." This was very polite conversation—too polite. I wanted to bare souls with this man I'd idolized since I was fourteen. Impatience had taken over, and my leg began to shake.

"Do you like Key West?" Tennessee asked.

"Yes, this place feels like gay paradise. How long have you

lived here?" I wanted to get inside his head; that's where the answers were. The boys at our table fidgeted petulantly; they wanted more attention from him. He ignored them.

"Since 1949, but I visited here for years before that. I've seen it change a lot."

I was just born when he moved here. At that time, *The Glass Menagerie* was already a huge success. He was at the threshold of his greatest work. I felt intimidated. How could I think I could relate to this man, that I could talk to him about my life dilemma? "What do you do here?" I asked. I knew his answer would have to mention something about his work. Perhaps that would be a segue into a deeper conversation. The music swelled, bodies were sweat-drenched and nearly naked, too much to distract us. I wanted to leave with him, go somewhere to talk.

"I write." He laughed loudly, making me think of Big Daddy from *Cat on a Hot Tin Roof*.

I turned stage right to see Sebastian bringing my cognac. We flashed smiles at each other as he handed me the drink. I read something in his face. Was he flirting? He oozed sensuality. Why did Tennessee ask him to get my drink? Was he the chosen boy at the time? I turned my attention back to Tennessee. "Are you working on anything now?"

"Oh, I'm always working on something. Yes, I am." He was grinning at me. Something was on his mind.

"A play?" I asked enthusiastically, knowing what the answer would be.

"Yes, a couple of plays. I'll be opening one in Chicago soon."

"Chicago! That's where I live." This was another thread weaving us together. I knew that meant he would have to be in Chicago sometime. Perhaps we would start a conversation that would continue after I left Key West. I was ready for anything.

"Cold, too windy, not very pretty, but Chicago has been good to me." I knew he'd premiered some of his best work there.

"It's the only home I've known," I responded humbly.

"You've never lived anywhere else?" he asked incredulously.

"I've traveled a lot but never lived anywhere else."

"I've traveled my entire life, never liked being home with the family or in any one place for very long—Key West is the only place I've called home." Again, he looked strangely frightened, his face partly in shadow, as if he were recalling a bad memory. He quickly changed the subject. "You look Italian."

"I'm Sicilian and Neapolitan."

"Well, that's Italian." He laughed loudly.

I had read he was fond of Italians and Italy. "Italians think of Sicilians as 'mixed blood,' not true Italian," I quizzically replied.

He laughed again, as if I shared something familiar with him. "The love of my life was Sicilian."

"Frankie Merlo?"

"Yes, Frankie, a beautiful boy." Frankie had died of lung cancer in 1963, sending Tennessee into a drug and alcohol haze for much of the 1960s. "You remind me of Frankie. He didn't have your eyes, though. Those don't look like Sicilian eyes."

I was flattered. My eyes are blue-gray and, at that time, framed by thick, black curly hair. "My mother is the Sicilian, but she has red hair, light skin, and blue-gray eyes. I think she has Norman blood. That's where the blue eyes come from."

"Would you come home with me?"

His request caught me off guard. Did he want to have sex with me? That was not in my script. I was in uncharted waters. Nervously, I inquired, "What for?" It felt defensive to ask that question.

"I enjoy talking with you. I thought we could continue our conversation in a more comfortable environment."

I assumed that by "comfortable environment," he meant his home and not his bed. How could I refuse Tennessee Williams? "I'd like that," I replied awkwardly. I couldn't have sex with my hero. I wasn't attracted to him that way. But I decided to take him at his word. After all, we were going to have the conversation I'd been hoping for in the comfort of his home. I couldn't ask for more.

He looked very pleased that I would accompany him home. He found his sandals and rose from the table. Sebastian and a young actor named Alexander joined us. Alexander had teeth like a strand of pearls and eyes like garnets that twinkled brightly in Tennessee's light ... *twinkle, twinkle, little star.*

Alexander extended his hand and dramatically announced, "Mr. Williams, it's a pleasure to meet you," as he bowed. I imagined he had a feathered Cyrano de Bergerac hat in his hand. The three of us escorted Tennessee down the stairs, Alexander on his left, I on his right, and Sebastian leading the way. The cast was assembled for Act I, scene 2: famous sailor, would-be actor, Viking stud, and me, idol worshiper. As we descended the sacred stairs, Alexander chattered on. "Did you have a good time tonight? I thought the place was too crowded. Crowds make me uncomfortable. Have you seen my play, Tennessee?"

We had begun our descent down the second flight of stairs as Tennessee turned to answer him. Coincidently, my travel companions—John, Duncan, Rick, and Bob—were flanking the staircase like guardian angels, heralding the way. I flashed a triumphant smile their way. They knew I'd admired this man for years and had missed my opportunity to meet him a year ago. Now, I was part of his entourage.

As Tennessee was turning to face Alexander, his right hand knocked into my arm, and my glass of cognac plummeted to the stone floor, where it shattered into a million pieces. Heads turned. We were in the spotlight.

"Did I do that?" Tennessee asked in amazement.

"It slipped out of my hand," I assured him.

The angels glared disapprovingly at the broken glass. Was this an omen? Ignoring the broken glass, we scurried out of the bar. Sebastian ran ahead to get the car. When he pulled up to the entrance, we squeezed into a small Toyota station wagon and sped off into the night.

"We need some champagne," Alexander said, still auditioning.

"And a bottle of mouthwash," Tennessee added.

It was 1:00 a.m. when we stopped at an all-night grocery store. Sebastian and Tennessee went to get the liquid requirements. Alexander and I waited in the car. Since he was able to keep a running dialogue going with himself, I was certain we would find a way to start a conversation.

"Do you live in Key West?" Alexander asked. He was familiar to me. I knew many young, eager, shallow wannabes, willing to do anything to accomplish the goal of becoming a recognized actor. But I liked him. Like me, he was determined to be an artist, and that redeemed him.

"Chicago." I was looking at him as I spoke. He was looking out the window. I think I made him nervous.

Without turning to face me, he said, "It's cold there."

"Only in the winter," I said. We both laughed. He was finally looking at me. It was the first opportunity I had to get a good look at him. He had thick, shiny, straight dark hair, cut in a girl's pageboy that framed his face, and beautiful, large, almond-shaped dark eyes. He had white, white skin and a boyish mien, but his constant chattering pushed him over the line into girlish.

"Yes, but I don't ever like to be cold. That's why I live here." He paused, threw his head back, and said, "And then there's always the theater." The line and gesture was Tallulah Bankhead, but without the whiskey-soaked voice, it sounded silly. He seemed more eager than ready to take his work seriously.

"So you're an actor?"

"I've been acting for six years, since high school." That put him at twenty-three years old. I was ten years older than he.

"Do you support yourself that way?" I knew he didn't; I wanted to know what his real job was.

"Well, I also wait tables. There isn't enough theater in Key West to keep me busy. I'm thinking about joining a traveling company." I respected him for pursuing theater instead of bar hopping.

Sebastian and Tennessee returned.

"This was the only champagne they had." Sebastian handed the bottle to Alexander.

"This is fine, as long as it bubbles and sparkles!"

Tennessee was clutching a small bottle of Scope. Of all the things he could have wanted at 1:00 a.m., why mouthwash? Was it something he needed, or did he think we would be kissing? Whatever his intention, it was funny.

Tennessee's home was a small white-frame cottage on a

double lot with a whitewashed gazebo off to the left. "TOM," which is Tennessee's real name, was carved into the railing. I was surprised at how humble the setting was. There was a coach house in the back, which I thought was his studio. I imagined him sitting there, night after night, writing some of the greatest plays of the twentieth century.

A heated swimming pool filled the second lot. I scanned the grounds. Dust covered everything. Overgrown plants, reclining lounge chairs, paper Chinese lanterns, half-filled glasses of wine, and torch lighting made it look like a set for one of his plays.

We walked through the house to the veranda where a riot of bougainvillea was entwined on trellises. A lazy bulldog greeted us and followed as we walked. As we entered the pool area, the piercing squawk of a fat cockatoo announced our arrival. A few large-winged palm trees lined the perimeter of the pool and several tattered Chinese lanterns, strung from tree to tree, spread dim light. A few votive candles flickered.

The stage was set. *It was* Suddenly, Last Summer, *and Violet Venable was escorting the doctor through her all-consuming garden while explaining how on the Encantadas, the newly hatched baby turtles race to the ocean to take their first swim in the nourishing mother sea, while vultures dive to tear open and eat their soft underbellies. The concerned doctor listens and is speechless ...* as was I.

"Let's sit around the pool," Alexander suggested. Tennessee was hurriedly moving in that direction in order to collapse into a chaise lounge in the center of the pool area. I was surprised at how ordinary the furniture looked. Inexpensive tubular steel tables and unstable plastic chairs with shabby old pillows looked like the kind bought at the local hardware store. We gathered around him, like understudies hoping to hear wisdom from our mentor.

Alexander found everything fascinating and made himself at home, as if he lived there. He busily moved chairs around so as to sit next to Tennessee. I sat on Tennessee's right, eagerly waiting for my next direction. The mood was changing. Tennessee was becoming seductive. He put his hand on my knee and morphed into Alexandra Del Lago, the princess. *It was Sweet Bird of Youth, and the princess wanted my attention. Insecure and afraid the best years of her career were over, she diverted her attention from her pain by being in the arms of an attractive young man. The princess had drunk a quart of gin and was in a playful mood. She wanted to be entertained.*

"I love to swim," Tennessee said, as he peered into my soul. "It's what keeps me alive. I've done it all my life; can't imagine not being near a pool." He turned to Sebastian. "Why don't you undress that young man and throw him into the pool?" He looked over at a frisky Alexander, who was eager to perform.

Sebastian quickly responded. He smiled at me like a boy playing a game with a friend. "Give me a hand, Tony." We had Alexander naked in seconds. Sebastian grabbed his hands; I, his legs, and with a triumphant toss, we threw him into the pool. When he came up for air, he made a graceful turn and glided across the water like a Busby Berkeley girl. This was his moment in the spotlight.

Tennessee continued to direct the scene, as Alexandra Del Lago might have. He hadn't taken his eyes off me. "Tony, let's see your body," he ordered nonchalantly, as if talking about the weather.

"I don't swim." At first, I was uncomfortable getting naked, but it was a Tennessee Williams production and sensuality was essential to the story.

"That's okay. I'd like to see what you look like." The moment morphed again.

We were the cabana boys in Night of the Iguana, *and Maxine was in charge of how this scene was played.* With that character in mind, it made it easier for me to perform for him. Once I entered the scene, I was ready and willing to get naked and play with the other cabana boys. Aerobics four times a week and light weight lifting made me confident that I was in good shape.

I slowly removed each piece of clothing. Tennessee gazed at me as if I were a private dancer. As I removed the last article of clothing, my underwear, he laughed.

"You're beautiful, Tony!"

My tanned Sicilian body was dramatically accentuated by my firm, round, baby-white ass, which I never exposed to the sun. I thought a tan line was sexier than an all-tanned body. With that, I got into the rhythm of the scene. I was Maggie the cat in *Cat on a Hot Tin Roof*. I knew how to please a man. *I'm alive! Maggie the cat is alive!* I triumphantly thought. "You're kind," I said modestly.

Tennessee was smiling at me like a horny sailor. "Why don't you go for a dip?" he seductively asked. I was naked and standing in front of him.

"I think I will too," Sebastian said with lustful enthusiasm. The Viking quickly undressed and jumped into the water. As I watched him flex his perfect physique, Tennessee stroked my rippling abs.

His hands moved over me like a gardener smoothing out the soil after planting seeds. "You have a good body." The cabana boys were frolicking in the water, and I was standing naked in front of Tennessee Williams as he stroked my body.

"Okay, here I go," I awkwardly announced and dove into the pool, treading water like a drowning cat to stay afloat. I splashed my way to one end and signaled Sebastian to come over. He seemed to be very familiar with this scene, and I had questions to ask him. The glow from the Chinese lanterns illuminated his chiseled body as he sliced through the water toward me. With the physique of a champion swimmer, he took to the water like a pro. Alexander was continuing a running monologue for anyone who would listen.

"So what's going on here?" I asked. I hoped he could give me a perspective on the scene and perhaps some advice.

Sebastian hungrily smiled at me and said, "He likes you. I can tell."

I scrutinized his sculpted face. He was cut from a block of pure white marble, like Michelangelo's David. "What do you mean?" I asked.

He clasped his hands behind his head and stretched his arms back like a champion weight lifter being photographed for the cover of a magazine. "I haven't seen him so animated in a long time."

"Well, what do you suppose he wants from me?" I asked.

"Conversation. He's lonely."

I instantly felt more relaxed. He winked at me and sped back across the pool to lift himself out of the water. The soft light from the lanterns made his wet body glow as he put on a white cotton robe. He was a god.

"How do you like my pool, Tony?" Tennessee reasserted himself into the scene.

I splashed across the pool and climbed out of the water. I grabbed a beltless robe, which caused me to clutch the front of it to keep from exposing myself. With new confidence, I sat next to Tennessee. Sebastian spread himself provocatively across a chaise lounge. I had to distract myself from staring at him. "The pool is refreshing. How often do you swim?" I asked Tennessee.

"I try to every day," he quickly responded. Our faces were very close; I could see he was beyond tired. His eyes were bloodshot, the skin around them red and swollen, and flickering candlelight deepened the lines on his wizened face. He was just an old man. It looked as if he was wearing a ceremonial devil mask.

Alexander had completed his water ballet. Still chattering, he exited the water and found a third robe. We three wet apostles gathered around our sage to await our next instruction.

"I love that tree." Tennessee pointed to his right. It was the tallest palm flanking the pool. "It dances delightfully." He was painting the backdrop for the next scene. Alexander poured champagne. Tennessee continued, "*I think that I shall never see a poem as lovely as a tree.*"

"Joyce Kilmer," I declared. I knew from my English teaching days what a bad piece of writing that was.

"That's an awful poem." He laughed and changed the focus. "*Shall I compare thee to a summer's day?*" He was looking at me.

Alexander picked up the line. "*Thou art more lovely and more temperate.*"

Tennessee: "*Rough winds to shake the darling buds of May.*"

Alexander: "*And summer's lease hath all too short a date.*"

I had memorized that Shakespeare sonnet in college and wanted to get in on the oral recitation. I picked it up:

"Sometime too hot the eye of heaven shines,

And often is his gold complexion dimmed,

And every fair from fair declines,

By chance or Nature's changing course untrimmed."

Tennessee attempted the next line. *"But thy time ...* No, wh—"

I continued as he faltered:

"But thy eternal summer shall not fade,

Nor lose possession of that fair thou ow'st,

Nor shall death brag thou wander'st in his shade,

When in eternal lines to time thou grow'st.

So long as men can breathe or eyes can see,

So long lives this, and this gives life to thee."

Tennessee applauded. "That's very good, Tony."

"Thank you, thank you." I proudly accepted his praise. Alexander poured the last of the champagne. Tennessee got up from his seat and moved to the recliner where I was stretched out. Without looking, he clumsily plopped himself down on top of me. It was like what a girlfriend might do when she's not getting enough attention from her boyfriend. I sipped the last of my champagne and struggled to sit still under his weight.

"Yes, that's a very beautiful tree. I love that tree," he casually continued the conversation as if to camouflage his abrupt move.

Alexander tried to regain the spotlight. "It is a beautiful tree. I love it too."

"Frank loved that tree," Tennessee said somberly. His cheerful spirit slipped away when he mentioned Frank. The tree was somehow infused with Frankie's spirit.

I wondered what else the palm tree had witnessed in the days before Frank's death. I imagined naked young men, lounging around the pool, partying with Tennessee and Frank, basking in the light of this famous couple. With Frank gone, the setting was neglected, yet the tree remained as a constant reminder of his time with Frank.

"Did he?" asked Alexander.

Before Tennessee could answer, Sebastian, knowing the scene had changed again, interjected, "I think we'd better be going."

Alexander looked surprised and disappointed. "Oh, all right." Reluctantly, he began to dress. Sebastian was dressed in an instant. He moved over to where Tennessee and I were reclining.

"See you tomorrow, Tennessee." Sebastian smiled.

"Yes," Tennessee responded. He was focused on me as Sebastian bent down to give me a full, wet kiss. I was surprised he did that right under Tennessee's nose, but I liked it.

"See you sometime." He winked.

"I'll be in Key West a while longer," I said, to let him know I was interested and available.

Alexander gave Tennessee a hug, saying, "This has been such a pleasure. I really enjoyed meeting you. Come see my play. I hope I see you again. Thanks so much." His delivery was swift as they exited stage right.

As soon as they were gone, Tennessee burst into tears. He sobbed as if he was in great pain. I was startled and waited for him to speak.

"I'm very lonely, you know." He sounded so sad. Tears poured down his cheeks. Where was this coming from? At first, I thought he was acting, but he sobbed uncontrollably, like a child needing comforting. He really was distressed.

I didn't know what to do. I had to say something. "We're all alone." I attempted to turn his sadness into something philosophical.

He continued with despair. "I have nobody. I've met nothing but con men since Frank died. I just want a little companionship, someone I can trust. Will you stay the night?"

I wanted to take his pain away, but how could I possibly give him what he needed? I was confused. The difference between the idol in my mind and the sad old man before me was palpable. I couldn't understand how Tennessee Williams could be so sad after he'd accomplished so much. How could he not be basking with pride in the glory of his achievements? Later, I would learn that his sadness was from something much, much deeper.

I had to comfort him, but I didn't know how. I was worried what spending the night would mean. What would I have to do to comfort him?

"Um ... why?" I tried to be gentle, compassionate.

"I'd like you to put me to bed and talk to me while I fall asleep." Tears continued pouring down his bright red face. He was begging to be taken care of. I had no choice but to help.

"Okay, I'll stay." It wasn't much to ask. He got up from the chaise we were sharing and shuffled to his bedroom. The lazy bulldog and I followed.

Black velvet drapes covered the bedroom window. A desk was strewn with papers, manuscripts, and a typewriter. Tabletops were cluttered with dishes, cups, glasses, and plastic pill bottles. The dresser displayed photographs and more pill bottles. He walked into the closet to grab a handful of yet more pill bottles. He walked over to the bed and dropped them.

"Could you find the Valium for me?"

There were so many bottles to search through, some half -full, some empty. I found the Valium after searching through dozens of empty vials. Why did he keep all these vials? How did he find his medication when he was alone?

"How many?" I asked.

"Two, please, with some water." I brought him the water and the two Valium. He quickly swallowed them and collapsed onto the bed, fully dressed. "I am very lonely, Tony."

Again, I didn't know how to respond. Awkwardly, I sat next to him on the bed. I began to realize that there was so much about this man I didn't know or understand, yet he was opening his heart and soul to me. My thirty-three years hadn't yet revealed how painful life could be. I felt unqualified to comfort him. He needed someone who understood the human heart as he did.

"I like you. Are you with anyone?" he asked, tear-drenched and garbled.

I appreciated his directness. It was how I usually interacted with people. It was easy to talk with him. I gathered that he found me different from the young men he usually met, and I was flattered. "No. I broke up with a partner a year ago," I said.

"How long were you together?"

"About six years." Kerry had been the first man I was with and my first love. Six years older than me, he provided stability during the turbulent, uncertain years when I was struggling to be a filmmaker. At first, we were very happy together. As time went on, we learned we were very different from one another. I was outgoing and spontaneous. He liked to stay home and read. We grew apart and finally separated. I hadn't been serious about anyone since.

"Frank and I were together thirteen years, the best years of my life." He paused to look directly into my eyes. "I'm going to die, you know."

Again, I was caught off guard by this sudden turn. I didn't know if he meant he had a terminal disease, or if he thought he didn't have much time left because of his age. I couldn't understand his grief. I speculated; the best of his life was behind him—his triumphs in theater, his life with Frankie, his relationships with the most talented and famous people in the world. Where was the glory? Why were there no close friends by his side? Why were there only con men who fed off him like vampires? The emptiness left by the losses he endured seemed inordinately great.

In the last scene of Williams's *Night of the Iguana*, Nonno, the dying old poet, emerges from his year-long writing incubation to take his last breaths of life while reciting his last poem before he dies. The last four lines are:

Oh courage! Could you not as well
Select a second place to dwell
Not only in that golden tree
But in the frightened heart of me.

It is a perfect Tennessee Williams dramatic scene. Nonno's niece is holding his wheelchair to steady him. The rest of the cast and crew are perched to listen, speechless in the presence of the dying poet.

I felt I had Nonno in my arms that night. I tried to be gentle. The only words I could say were, "We're all going to die." Trite but true; I began to stroke his hair.

"I'm going to die soon. My body doesn't want to carry me anymore."

I moved closer to him and let the warmth of my body engulf him. He began to relax into my arms. I embraced him like a mother putting a child to bed.

"I don't want to die alone," he said, sobbing. I cradled him tighter and rocked back and forth. I didn't know how to rescue someone from despair. "Will you stay here? There's an adjoining room on the other side of the toilet. You can sleep there." The request seemed innocent enough. It was the least I could do for my world-worn hero.

"Yes, I'll stay." I felt that I was in way over my head. Nothing prepared me for this. I was becoming part of the tragedy he was living. Like Shannon, the defrocked minister in *Night of the Iguana*, I was being drawn into a drama I didn't need or want.

"I'll be all right, knowing you're in the next room." The tears were gone and a smile returned to his face. A little affection and a warm body temporarily made him feel safe. He kissed me on the cheek and gently unfastened my jeans. "Do you mind?" I wanted to say please stop, but he was already pulling down my jeans. I couldn't pull away. He was so sad, so needy. I said nothing.

He opened my zipper, reached in for my penis, and began to suck it. I felt detached from my body. This wasn't sexual. It was more like a feeding. I felt I had let myself down. "Thank you, baby. I don't expect you to do the same for me." He'd had his warm milk and was ready to sleep.

I felt used and helpless. I was caught in his spell. I caressed him until he fell asleep and then got up and went into the adjoining bedroom. I must have been asleep for two or three hours when I heard the door of my room open. In the dim morning light, I could see his body silhouetted in the doorway. He stared down at me. I lifted my head and looked up at him. He backed out of the room. I think he wanted to know that I'd kept my promise to stay the night.

I got up at 9:00 a.m., dressed, and walked into the living room. Like his bedroom, it was strewn with glasses, papers, books, and manuscripts. Bookshelves flanked the room and were filled with books. Maria Callas's albums took up an entire shelf. I imagined Frankie lying here, listening to her glorious voice blasting *Vissi d'arte* from 78 rpms of vinyl.

To the left of the bookcase was a signed photograph of Eugene O'Neill, to the right a signed photograph of T. S. Eliot. I stepped closer to examine Eliot's signature. It was the same hand that wrote *The Love Song of J. Alfred Prufrock, The Wasteland,* and *The Hollow Men,* all of which I worshiped. My eyes scrutinized his face, his hands, his signature. I imagined Williams, O'Neill, and Eliot, sitting in this room, talking about the human condition. I wanted to hear that conversation, to learn from the masters. I could feel their spirits here in this tattered room.

The bulldog followed me around like a sentinel. Tennessee was still asleep. I didn't know what to do. Should I write a note and leave? Should I wake him? I decided to wake him. I gently turned the knob of his bedroom door. It was locked.

"Tennessee?" I could hear him moving.

"Tony?" I heard him get out of bed. "Wait a minute, baby."

He was fumbling to open the door. Groggy, disheveled, and with a ruby satin Big Daddy robe draped around his body, he smiled at me. Light poured into the dark space of his bedroom. Without stepping out, he said, "Have something to eat."

"No, thank you." The play was over. It was time to leave. "Sorry to wake you." I could see the white sailor suit crumpled on the floor near his bed. A night with Tennessee Williams and some of his most indelible characters that sprang from him like spirits: Violet, Alexandra, Maxine, the cabana boys, and Nonno. It was a dream come true but different than I had imagined it. "I think I'll be leaving and wanted to thank you. This has been a treasure." I'd misspoken. "I mean, pleasure," I corrected myself, though treasure was more accurate.

"I'd like to see you for dinner tonight."

It was my last night in Key West. It would be my last chance to play with friends before we left. "I can't for dinner. How about afterwards?"

"Yes, okay. Meet me at the Monster at midnight."

"Okay." I stood, waiting for my cue to leave.

"Tony, can I see you when I'm in Chicago?"

"Sure, that would be great!" I was elated. The conversation would continue as I'd hoped.

"Yes, I'd like that very much too." He pointed to a table outside his bedroom where a pad of paper and a pen lay.

"I'll write my address and phone number so you can call when you're in town," I said.

"Yes, you do that. Leave it on the desk there. Now I have to sleep." He backed into his bedroom and got back into bed. I stepped into the fractured bedroom light. As he dozed off, I bent to kiss him on the cheek. Quietly, I left the room, closed the door, wrote down my contact information, and walked out of the house.

The Key West morning was blazing bright white. I took off my shirt to feel the salty, warm ocean breeze. Flowers and trees were flames of color in the early morning light, the air sweet. As I walked back to the compound, the tiny resort town slowly came to life. Everything was the same but different. I had sprouted wings.

When I arrived back at the Lighthouse Court, my friends were gathered poolside, having breakfast—all the guardian angels waiting for the return of the prodigal son. We spent our last day doing our usual routines: breakfast poolside, afternoon shopping, nap time, fashionably late dinner. I arrived at the Monster at 11:45 p.m. and eagerly looked around for TW—12:15, 12:30, 1:00 a.m. came but still no Tennessee. I hoped there would be another scene, but perhaps, I told myself, the script was completed. His absence didn't bother me. I was content to live in the afterglow of my one-night adventure with my literary hero. Perhaps I would see him in Chicago. As I was about to leave the Monster, Sebastian walked up to me.

"I thought I'd find you here." He smiled at me as if I were a luscious piece of meat he was about to devour.

"I was supposed to meet Tennessee here, but he didn't show up."

"I'm not surprised. He often forgets his commitments. I wouldn't take it personally. I could tell he liked you. You'll hear from him again."

"I hope so. I have admired him for years."

"Is that what you call it?" He smirked at me.

"What do you mean?" I asked.

"Oh, nothing. Tennessee knows a lot of people and has all different kinds of relationships," he said with confidence.

"Well, all I am interested in is getting to know him—a friendship," I said sincerely.

"Sure." He smirked again, as if he knew something I didn't. "So what are you doing tonight?" Sebastian asked with lust in his eyes.

"I came here with friends to wait for Tennessee, like I said," I replied with a coy smile. It was my last night in paradise. Sex with Sebastian would be a perfect ending to a great story.

"Why don't we go back to my place?" There was victory in his tone. I'd expected the proposition. Sebastian was impossible to resist. He exuded confidence and sensuality.

"Let me tell my friends I'm leaving. I'll be at the entrance in a few minutes," I said.

As I waited for Sebastian, I thought of Tennessee's book, *The Roman Spring of Mrs. Stone*. In the book, the young men come calling for the rich, older women, like cats lining up to service the felines in heat. Seductive and charming, the con men prey on the women's vulnerabilities and desperation. They are hustlers, looking for an all-expenses-paid night on the town, and afterward, they would expect to be paid for the fake romance they provided. Was Sebastian one of them?

"How do you know TW?" I asked him.

"Everyone who lives in Key West eventually gets to know him." He was flippant. I began to understand how succumbing to people who misrepresent their intentions could become a way of life in a small town with little to do. The artist, who in his work expressed truth and insight about the human condition, was in the end surrounded by liars. If Sebastian was representative of the people TW was surrounded with, I better understood his comment about "being surrounded by con men since Frankie died." Although Sebastian was powerfully seductive, I suspected he had little substantive to offer. He was more interested in what he could get.

As soon as we arrived at his place, Sebastian started kissing and undressing me. He quickly removed his clothes. Two hours later, I left, satisfied and exhausted. We made no plans to see each other again. This was Key West of the early 1980s, after all.

I left the next day. Upon returning home, I sent Tennessee a thank-you note, expressing my appreciation for the serendipitous encounter at the Monster. A week later, I received the first of several letters from him.

Letter #1: It goes, it goes ...

1432 Duncan St
Key West, 33040

March 8, 1982

Dear Tony:

I was so pleased to get your card today. I dread Chicago, so goddam
cold, those lake winds, and even though I feel I've created a good
play for the Goodman, I shall need a warm Sicilian friend there. Please
come to the 'intimate little birthday party' the Goodman is giving me
on March 26th.

I do have a better long play than the one to be done at The Goodman,
but I think it's for England or even Australia. You see, I plan to
use my passport a lot in the coming months. Did I tell you this?
I lived and travelled with a Sicilian for fourteen years, the only
truly happy years of my life.

I know the limitations imposed on me by time and this dreadful, though
lucrative, profession that I've been in since 1940.

Do you know the writing of Katharine Anne Porter? I had a crush on her
in the early Forties. She gave me her picture - she was a beautiful woman.
And we corresponded a while. I remember her last letter to me, in 1943.
I had enquired how she was faring and she wrote me back this delicate and
slightly cryptic response: 'It goes, it goes.'

A beautifully reticent way of describing an always difficult life.

I do my writing late at night. Afterwards, I get off this sort of
gimpy letter. But it goes, it goes...

With my love,

Tennessee

(Tom)

Letter #1

1432 Duncan St.

Key West, FL 33040

March 8, 1982

Dear Tony:

I was so pleased to get your card today. I dread Chicago—so god damn cold, those lake winds—and even though I feel I've created a good play for the Goodman, I shall need a warm Sicilian friend there. Please come to the "intimate little birthday party" the Goodman is giving me on March 26.

I do have a better long play than the one to be done at the Goodman, but I think it's for England or even Australia. You see, I plan to use my passport a lot in the coming months. Did I tell you this? I lived and traveled with a Sicilian for fourteen years, the only truly happy years of my life.

I know the limitations imposed on me by time and this dreadful though lucrative profession that I've been in since 1940.

Do you know the writing of Katharine Anne Porter? I had a crush on her in the early forties. She gave me her picture—she was a beautiful woman. And we corresponded a while. I remember her last letter to me, in 1943. I had inquired how she was faring and she wrote me back this delicate and slightly cryptic response: "It goes, it goes."

A beautifully reticent way of describing an always difficult life.

I do my writing late at night. Afterwards, I get off this sort of gimpy letter. But it goes, it goes ... With my love,

Tennessee

(Tom)

I was delighted to receive the letter and excited that the adventure would continue. I was also a bit wary; he was unpredictable and needy. Receiving this letter made me begin to think he was interested in more than friendship. Perhaps it was the Frankie Merlo connection, or perhaps he saw me as the companion he was looking for. Whatever the case, I was dancing on butterfly wings.

CHAPTER 2

A TASTE OF STARDOM

CHICAGO: MARCH 1982

I was asleep when the phone began to ring at 1:00 a.m. I had to be at work by 7:00. How irritating that someone would be calling me so late. Three weeks back from Key West, my tan and the encounter with TW were fading. I'd told the story of a flight of stairs, a barefooted sailor, and the kindness of a stranger many, many times. I'd started a journal to remember each detail of that special night with my hero. Meeting him also made me think more seriously about returning to film. Memories of wanting to be an artist continuously flashed in my mind.

My artistic pursuits began at the age of nine, when I asked my parents for piano lessons. I was smitten by the heavenly sound of a black grand piano. *Moonlight Sonata* and *For Elise* lifted my spirit before I knew what spirit was. My parents thought I was too young to know what I wanted to do with my life, so instead, I got accordion lessons. In their minds, an accordion was a grand piano sideways. After two months of taking tortuous organ grinder, lessons, I threw the accordion down the flight of stairs to the stone floor of the foyer of our apartment building, where it shattered into a million pieces. My parents thought this was proof positive that I didn't want to play the piano.

At the age of eleven, I watched *The Garry Moore Show* every week with my mother. I loved how the dancers flew through the air like birds. I wanted to fly like them and would dance across the living room floor in front of her to impress her with my innate talent. At first, she raved about my amazing ability to flap and fly back and forth across the living room.

"Anthony, you dance so well!" She was always supportive, and that was all the encouragement I needed. Each week, I would perform my avian ritual until I was exhausted. After weeks of my avid new interest, she got irritated and told me to stop.

"Anthony, stop it! I can't watch my show! Why don't you go play with something?"

I was crushed. My second artistic attempt was rejected.

Dancing not only lifted my spirit but also engaged my soul. I felt connected to the life force. As I got older, dancing became an essential part of my life. In my twenties, I would dance myself into a sweaty frenzy at clubs and bars across the country.

In high school, I fell in love with literature. I was fascinated with how it translated everyday life into something meaningful. *The Good Earth* woke up my appreciation for the significance of literature as an art form. Although set in China, Pearl S. Buck's story of Wang Lung's family's struggle for survival was my family's struggle for survival. Like the Lungs we were a poor, working class family, struggling just to get by.

I first encountered Tennessee Williams as a high school sophomore. *The Glass Menagerie* and Tom Wingfield's frustration with his family was my frustration. My parents didn't understand my sensitive, artistic nature. Laura's glass menagerie taught me how fragile and vulnerable we are. Amanda showed me how selfish and deluded we can be. I identified with Tom's restlessness and his desire to be an artist. Williams made literature understandable to me and part of my life for the rest of my life.

In college, as an English literature major, I kept a journal of my life's experiences. I wanted to be a writer of great literature, just like my hero, Tennessee Williams. I studied painting, sculpture, music, dance, theater. The arts were at the center of my life, and I passionately pursued all of them. However, it was film that seized my imagination most because it animated literature. I studied Fellini, Bergman, Truffaut, Chaplin, Welles, and more. The flickering images flashed in my soul like downloading software.

Fellini's *La Dolce Vita* was the first film that leapt off the

41

screen and into my psyche. I felt the ennui and isolation of those characters. I identified with Marcello's inability to commit to anyone. Like him, I was just meandering through life, looking for something to commit to, looking for something to believe in. Bergman's stark landscape in *Persona* showed me how empty life could be. *Citizen Kane* taught me how innocence is corrupted by power and greed. I wanted to interpret life through the medium of film.

I got a bachelor's degree in literature and a master's degree in writing and directing film. I made a film called *Brunch* that won best in show at Columbia College's student film festival. In my second year, I began a documentary about a painter who was having great anxiety over going from a private life to a public one as an artist. The film would chronicle her journey in her own words. It was going to be my debut into the film world. I was poised to make my childhood dreams come true.

One day toward the end of shooting, I went to my film locker to find the film's soundtrack gone. This was tragic because her voice was to tell the story of her journey—no voice, no film. All the days spent recording her voice were lost. To this day, I don't know if I lost it or if it was stolen. I never finished the project and was devastated by the loss. Losing the soundtrack felt like an amputation. There was no money, no resources, and no time to replace it. After weeks of angst, I had to let it go.

Coincidentally, at that same time a friend asked me if I

was interested in part-time work as a trainer for Xerox. Since I needed to reevaluate my future as a filmmaker, I succumbed to the seduction of earning $1,200 a month working in the business world. In 1978, I thought that was a fortune. At the same time, I knew I was just clocking time until I returned to film, but the money paid bills. The dilemma between art and business burned in my soul. I tried to find work in film: ad agencies, the Catholic archdioceses, film schools, freelance film companies, production houses. After a year of ruminating and little work, I feared that if I didn't take action soon, the flame would burn out forever. Leaving my film career was my first great loss in life. That was when I first experienced depression and anxiety. I considered moving to Los Angeles to take my chances knocking on film directors' doors, asking for work, but I didn't think I could be one of the thousands of eager young filmmakers who was looking for film work in LA. Then fate stepped in. It was during this time I met my first male partner, Kerry. I chose my love for him over my love of film and sadly didn't move to LA ... but the flame was still smoldering.

The Xerox job took up most of my time, and I was uninspired and discontented. The business world was dull, unimaginative and populated with drones who did what they were told. Management espoused its commitment to helping people learn and grow, but everything was really driven by "numbers" which was code for dollars. We were required to provide monthly projections on how much business we would close. Each quarter, senior management grilled us in front of our peers on how well we were building business. One by one, we would get up in front of the entire regional staff and answer questions on how we were working our territories. Some questions were relevant to our work, and others were designed to trip us up. They were looking for weakness. They referred to these weaknesses as "coaching opportunities."

If they didn't like our answer, we would be told what to do differently. This was considered a motivational approach to developing our consulting ability. They believed by making us feel we were on the verge of failure, we would be driven to succeed. It was a medieval approach to management. Collaboration was emphasized but never exercised. We were referred to as a team, but in truth, everyone was out for himself. Success was measured by who had the highest numbers. Teamwork was code for "be competitive." Do better than the other team members, and you'll be rewarded.

In the film world, teamwork was quintessential to making a film. The success of a film depended on the synergy of each person's role being executed as perfectly as possible. A director was only as good as the cinematographer. The cinematographer needed a crew. The crews needed to collaborate. The actors needed a good script and a talented director to make the story interesting and believable. Collaboration was the glue that made a film work.

I slipped under management's radar at Xerox. I was smart and articulate. What I didn't know, I made up. The work was easy and the money was good, but I was bored. Most people talked too much and said very little. If someone was personable and confident, people believed that person was skilled. I was both.

My mother groomed me from childhood in the art of conversation, the power of wit, and the value in being good-natured. She knew how to start a conversation with anyone on any topic and was a master at making people feel comfortable and engaged. As her firstborn, I was an attentive student. With personality and confidence, there was no situation my mother couldn't handle. She was my first hero. She was invincible. My loving relationship with her was in stark contrast to TW's loveless relationship with his mother. I understood how insecure and vulnerable he felt, because he never felt a mother's love and perhaps didn't know how to have a reciprocal loving relationship.

The business routines were monotonous as well. Five days a week, every morning at 6:30, I would drive from my apartment in Chicago's Old Town neighborhood to Arlington Heights, a northwest suburb. I would arrive early, greet the other eager, dedicated neophytes, and sit at my desk, fueling the meaningless activities that drove the business machine.

Prospecting, making appointments, customer sales calls, and closing business was the routine. Money ruled, and greed was its devoted servant. I played along because it was easy to be average. I was most confident when I had no idea what I was doing.

So here I was, at 1:00 a.m., dreading work and angry, and someone calling me at this hour. I let the phone ring several times, thinking it would stop. It persisted, and I was pissed.

"Hello," I responded in my most petulant tone

"Hello, is Tony there?" The voice was unfamiliar.

"This is he!" I said angrily.

"Tony, this is Scott. Tennessee would like to speak with you." I later would learn that Scott was TW's live-in valet. He took care of TW, making sure his professional commitments were made.

"What? Oh, yeah, okay ..." My petulance instantly dissolved into humility.

"Hi, baby! How are you?" TW laughed in his Big Daddy way.

"Fine. How are you?" I was elated he called me, even if it was 1 a.m.

"Yes, good, good. I would appreciate it if you would be my guest for a preview of my new play, *A House Not Meant to Stand*. It will be tomorrow at 8:00 p.m. at the Goodman Theatre. We could have a little dinner before we go. How does that sound?"

"Yes, I'd love to. What should I do?" I was out of bed pacing the floor. It was so exciting to get a phone call from him!

"Meet us at my hotel, the Delaware Towers, at 6:30. I have my own suite there. They are very good to me. We'll go from there."

"Okay, see you then." I was thrilled. I knew from his letter that he would be in town, but I had no idea when.

Act II of the adventure had begun.

The card and picture I sent him must have sealed his interest. However, I think he saw the adventure as more than just friendship. I was in awe of his genius but didn't want a romantic or sexual relationship with him. I was confident we could work things out.

It was 6:25 when I arrived at the Delaware Towers. I brought a bottle of champagne to celebrate TW's new play.

A guard at the front door greeted me. "May I help you?" he asked.

"Mr. Williams's suite, please?" I nervously asked.

"Oh, he just left."

"He did? Did he say where he was going?" I was stunned. Just like the last night in Key West, he wasn't where he said he would be.

"Who are you?" The doorman was doing his job. Who the hell was I, asking for the famous playwright?

"Um … Tony Narducci." I didn't get it. I knew I was on time.

"Oh, Mr. Narducci. Mr. Williams left you this note."

The note was scribbled on a small piece of scratch paper:

Dear Tony—Meet us at the Goodman Theater, 200 S. Columbus Drive, if you can. We had to go ahead.

Tennessee

Note from TW to meet at Goodman Theatre

Dear Tony —

meet us at
Goodman
Theatre, 200
S. Columbus
Drive, if you
can.

we had to
go ahead

Tennessee

I rushed out the door and found a cab, wondering how our communication had been misunderstood. "The Goodman, please. I'm in a hurry." The driver got me there in record time. I raced into the empty foyer of the Goodman. One lone usher stood by the entrance.

"Is Mr. Williams here?" I asked anxiously.

"Mr. Williams?" He looked confused.

"Tennessee Williams."

"Oh, ah, no, he isn't." He didn't seem to know whom I was asking about.

"When will he be here?"

"I don't know." I was barking up the wrong tree. It was clear that the lone usher was clueless. I decided to follow the sound of voices I could hear in the distance.

"What time does the performance begin?"

"Eight o'clock."

It was 6:50. There was plenty of time to find him and have a toast with the slightly chilled champagne. This was TW's night. I was sure he had more to do than wait for me.

I found my way to the bar and could see people scattered about in anticipation of a new Tennessee Williams play. I scanned the crowd but couldn't see TW. I hadn't eaten all day and was hungry. The only available sustenance was at the bar in liquid form.

"White wine, please." The bartender quickly delivered the sustenance. I guzzled it and had another. It was 7:45.

Duncan and Rick, the guardian angels who witnessed our exit from the Monster that first night, saw me sitting at the bar. What a coincidence they were here to witness Act II. Perhaps they really were guardian angels. We greeted, and I told them I was here with TW. Duncan told me they saw him at the far end of the bar.

I rushed to where Duncan indicated. There was TW, standing in the bar lounge outside of Ingrid's, the Goodman's lobby restaurant. He was with a very tall, younger man, whom I thought must be Scott. It would be hard to miss them. TW was about five foot six. Scott was nearly seven feet tall.

"Tennessee!" I shouted and waved the bottle of warm champagne.

He flashed his now familiar smile, but he looked anxious. A barricade of bodies stood between us. "Hi, baby!"

I burst through the crowd. He reached out and took my hand in both of his. It was a warm, gentlemanly welcome. I raised the bottle of champagne, and he smiled at it.

"What happened at the hotel?" he asked.

"I was there at 6:25 and just missed you."

"Why were you late?"

"I thought you said 6:30." I was sure he said 6:30, but it had been the middle of the night. Perhaps I had it wrong.

"I thought we said 6:00." He turned to Scott for agreement.

Scott said, "I don't remember." TW looked irritated with Scott.

I rescued us from an awkward moment. "Well, it's okay. I've had a few glasses of wine, and we're all here now."

There seemed to be tension between TW and Scott. Scott was a gentle but awkward-looking young man. I thought his height might contribute to that. He never looked at me. Maybe he and TW were lovers, and I was the "other" man. Scott didn't know I wasn't interested in playing that role.

"Yes, good." TW rolled his eyes in Scott's direction. I read it as blaming Scott for the misunderstanding.

Celebrity can't escape scrutiny. The crowd around us noticed we were discussing something, and they wanted to know what it was. Admirers constantly came up to TW, all of them with the same trite comments. They just wanted contact with the icon. He looked appreciative, in spite of hearing the same pointless comments over and over. I was beginning to understand the curse of celebrity.

"I've always admired your work, Mr. Williams," one would say.

"Thank you." He would smile. His public smile was different from the one I saw. He was performing here for his fans.

Then another would ask, "Mr. Williams, is this one as good as *Menagerie*?" How insensitive to ask him to compare his work. It was like asking, "Which of your children do you like best?"

People were careless. Their questions were stupid. This was why I couldn't approach him that first night at the Monster. I had nothing to say or ask that would be of interest to him. This was the sycophant syndrome: thoughtless interaction with a celebrity to make you feel better about yourself.

"I hope so, yes, I think so." He laughed loudly when people asked about the play. No question was annoying to him. He was enormously appreciative of the praise bestowed on him. What a showman. I loved watching him work the crowd.

The lights dimmed, and we entered the theater for *A House Not Meant to Stand*. This would be the last new TW play that would be mounted in his lifetime. We were joined by Bruce, who claimed to be a friend of Tennessee's. TW didn't like him. Bruce said he was in public relations. TW hadn't mentioned him to me, and he didn't work for the Goodman. I didn't know what he really did. He was aggressive, pushy, opinionated, and annoying. I instantly disliked him. He ignored me, which I appreciated.

The four of us sat together on the far right side of the theater: TW, Scott, me, and Bruce. TW was nervous and sat on the edge of his seat. He had Scott bring a copy of the manuscript in case he wanted to make changes.

TW talked and laughed out loud throughout the performance. He was having a conversation with the actors while they performed. Occasionally, he turned to one of us and rolled his eyes. At times, he would shake his head and say out loud, "No!" The production was his offspring. He was encouraging and reprimanding it like a father. I watched in awe as he gave it life. Like the Greek titan, Coronus, his children lived inside of him.

As soon as the lights came up for intermission, Scott ushered the three of us back stage. He sensed TW's anxiety, so we entered a small dressing room, and Scott quickly closed the door. TW burst into tears.

"It's a disaster!" He was genuinely, seriously upset. There

was no indication of this disaster before or during the performance. His reaction seemed out of proportion with what we'd seen. "The actors are all wrong. They don't understand the poetry. It's not holding together. I can't go back in there." Panic was in the air. It seemed something very bad had happened or would happen if the play continued. I wanted to help but had no idea what to do. Scott came to the rescue.

"Let's go to the lobby for a drink," Scott suggested.

I was surprised by how quickly TW acquiesced after being so upset. Later, he told me the fractured lineage of *A House Not Meant to Stand.* It began in November 1980 with the production of *Tennessee Laughs,* a compilation of three of his one-act plays performed in Goodman's little theater: *A Perfect Analysis Given by a Parrot, The Frosted Glass Coffin,* and *Some Problems for the Moose Lodge.* Encouraged by the Goodman's artistic director, Tennessee expanded *Moose Lodge* into a full production in 1981. It was ready to premiere in the Goodman's small theater on March 26, 1981. He revised the first production and then expanded it to get it ready for the large theater.

His rewrites dragged on. The Goodman was concerned it would not be ready for opening by March 1982. The play had three different directors, one of whom Tennessee had an affair with. All of this added more complications to the challenges of meeting the deadline.

Eventually, the Goodman staff and the director intervened and completed the play. TW was locked out of the theater as they "destroyed my poetry!" as he was known to say. The baby was snatched out of his hands by foster parents and cannibalized. He felt emotionally and artistically raped.

A House Not Meant to Stand was not captivating like his early work. It lacked continuity and insight. It seemed to me it was more a characterization of members of his family than a compelling story of contemporary life. Whether this was due to his aging creativity or the usurpers' pen was never clear to me. In fact, I never knew if his story was true. All that was clear was his misery over the production we were seeing.

I followed Scott and TW to the lobby. I didn't want to be caught by a camera. The lobby was filled with the chattering of eager admirers. When they saw TW, they flocked around him like sparrows jumping into a birdbath. He lit up. A glass of wine and his admiring public helped him put his sorrows aside. The adulation, the attention, was the good side of being a celebrity. Regardless of whether the play was good or not, people were just appreciative to see a new production by the great playwright. However, eventually the crowd would become a swarm, and TW would be devoured. I could see distress wash over his face as they engulfed him. Later, he told me it was enormously stressful for him to be in public. Questions about his work made him defensive. As more people invaded his space, fear and danger began to register on his face. Like Blanche in *A Streetcar Named Desire*, he survived through charm. It was a disguise he could hide behind, as he did with the sailor suit in Key West. Eventually, he was overwhelmed and he would search the crowd for a familiar face. Scott or I would come to the rescue.

Although I had begun the evening as an anonymous observer, I was transformed during the first act into a minor celebrity. The Goodman staff, the ushers, and the bartender suddenly knew my name. They smiled at me as we accompanied TW through the crowd. I was still clutching the now very warm bottle of champagne. The bartender went out of his way to approach me.

"Mr. Narducci, would you like to keep that champagne chilled?"

"Yes, thank you."

"I didn't know you were with Mr. Williams. I should have given you the wine for free."

"Oh, that's okay." Benevolence came easily to a celebrity, but I felt awkward. TW was still entwined with the admiring crowd. We were separated by the fray. An officious man and a young woman marched through the crowd toward me.

"Mr. Narducci, my name is Greg. I am the artistic director of the theater."

"Nice to meet you, Greg." I knew he was well-known for his work at the Goodman.

"This is my assistant, Sandra."

"Please call me Tony. How are you, Sandra?" I was becoming more and more important every minute.

"Fine, and you?" Her smile said "willing to accommodate."

"Fine." I wasn't sure how to play celebrity. Should I act aloof? Were inquisitiveness and politeness indicators of the lack of celebrity?

"Are you enjoying the play?" she asked, as if she were interviewing me. It was an innocuous opening question, but I could tell she wanted to get information. Who was I? Why was I here? What was my relationship with TW?

"Yes, very much," I replied with an air of authority, as if I had reflected on what she asked and had great insights to offer. "Are you?"

"Oh, I haven't seen it yet. There have been so many things to take care of. I'll get to it eventually."

I was surprised she hadn't seen it. I thought we were going to engage in a serious conversation about Act I, but she knew nothing about it. She was assistant to the artistic director but hadn't seen the play? How could she do the job? Before I could ask when she would see the play, she saw someone else she had to talk to and was off.

"Excuse me. Nice meeting you." She trotted away. Perhaps I wasn't as important as I was beginning to think.

People surrounded TW, making him inaccessible. I wandered among them, enjoying my new cloak of celebrity. Who did they think I was: businessman, agent, friend, companion? It didn't matter.

The lights flickered for Act II to begin. We brought our

cocktails into the theater. Scott smuggled a full bottle of wine for us to drink as well. TW occasionally laughed and made comments to Scott, but nothing was written down on the script. In spite of his disappointment, he didn't make any changes. This didn't make sense to me. So much drama in what "didn't work" but nothing put into making it better. It seemed the flame of his creative passion had burned out. He was in automatic drive now. The words of the play were put to paper, but the soul of the play was buried in the exaggerated drama. It saddened me to think he was only a shell of his former pulsating genius.

We finished the wine as Act II came to an end. The audience applauded vigorously. The lights came up, and people clamored to congratulate TW. He didn't say much. A plastered smile warded off worship.

In the lobby, Aaron Gold, who had a celebrity column in the *Chicago Sun Times*, came up to TW and asked if he would answer a couple of questions. TW could barely respond before he was ushered into a dining room, where a film crew had been set up. He was led to center stage for light readings and sound takes. Aaron fussed over him. I was amazed at how quickly and efficiently all this happened.

Aaron was doing his job. He was determined to get the exclusive on the new Tennessee Williams play. TW loved the publicity. I watched him transform from a tired, beleaguered playwright into a celebrity. Protecting his "children" from the voracious public galvanized him. His plays were supreme beings. They gave him strength. They gave him power. Otherwise, he was weak and vulnerable.

He looked fresh and ready to take on the scrutiny of an expert interviewer. I gazed in awe at all of this. Witty spontaneity was the key to maintaining celebrity status. A young woman with a pad of paper and pen in hand came up to me. I could tell she was part of Aaron's team.

"Who are you?" she asked in a condescending way.

"A friend of Tennessee's. Who are you?" I wasn't going to capitulate to a kid with a clipboard.

"The producer. You'll have to leave." She couldn't have been ruder.

"I think I'd better stay."

She turned center stage. "Aaron, this guy thinks he should stay. Is it okay?" She pointed her pen at me with disdain. Aaron looked at TW.

He flashed his smile at me, beaming. "Oh yes, Tony must stay."

Aaron had the last word. "It's fine," Aaron said uncaringly to the producer.

I waved her away as if she were a mosquito buzzing around my ear. She left as rudely as she entered. My confidence grew. What she and others didn't understand is that TW wanted protection from the onslaught of a careless public. Celebrity was a magnet. People were drawn to it without consideration for the vulnerabilities of the man behind the mask.

Eventually, everything was ready for shooting. The room was dark except for a bright light that shined on TW. Aaron started.

"Tell us about *A House Not Meant to Stand.*" Aaron was most earnest.

"What do you want to know?" TW asked. He chuckled before and after he answered each question. He had been through this routine before. He let Aaron define what he was asking. Aaron got more specific.

"How does it compare to your other work?" This was the question TW disliked most.

"Oh, I suppose it is as good as anything else I've done. I am older now, you know." TW laughed at his stating the obvious. He was composed, articulate, lucid, and interesting. They went back and forth about *A House*. Tennessee was engaging, nonspecific, and always cheerful.

Aaron got to the big question of the night. "Do you think you are the greatest living American playwright?"

TW laughed loudly. Whether he answered yes or no, it was an indictment. I was uncomfortable for him. TW turned the question back to Aaron. "I don't know. What do you think?"

Aaron was less skillful in the chess game of life. TW didn't let his ego speak. Aaron had to answer his own question. He made a gratuitous comment. "I think most people would say you are a contender."

TW smiled victoriously.

The interview went on for a half hour. When it was over, the tone changed. Aaron's work was done. Smiles were put to rest. A couple of handshakes and we were asked to exit to the left. Back in the lobby, Greg came up to us.

"You must stop at the cast party. They've been waiting for you in the lobby bar."

"Yes, we must." TW looked back to see that I was following. I could tell he didn't want to go to the party, but he wanted to express his appreciation to the cast for their work. A few stragglers were waiting to meet the famous playwright. As we entered, a woman lurched at him.

"Oh, Mr. Williams, I think we have a success!"

Another quickly added, "Mr. Williams, I love my part!"

And another: "Mr. Williams, this is our *Streetcar*!" Like birds chirping, they talked simultaneously. TW smiled but didn't answer.

His mood ran up and down throughout the evening. We stayed a short time, made excuses, and exited. Back in the lobby, an usher came up to us with a note. Scott read it.

"We have to meet Bruce at the restaurant Biggs. He's arranged a late dinner with Robert Falls."

"Oh yes. Good. I want to meet that young man."

Robert Falls had recently directed *A Streetcar Named De-*

sire at Wisdom Bridge Theatre in Chicago. The production was still being performed, and TW told his publicist he wanted to meet the director while he was in Chicago. TW had recently seen it and was very impressed with Falls's work. He complimented the production by saying it was the best he had seen in a long time and encouraged a meeting between him and Robert. Bruce was determined to make this a significant event and got the owner of Biggs to make the restaurant available for this special meeting.

We were off into the night. Biggs was an old-fashioned restaurant located in one of the few surviving Gold Coast mansions from the turn of the century. The cast of characters for the private late dinner was assembled for a talented young director and a brilliant playwright to meet.

We arrived at the restaurant at 1:00 a.m. I hadn't eaten all day. Still carrying the bottle of champagne, I followed Scott and TW into Biggs. Bruce was there with open arms and a cartoon smile.

Dressed in late Victorian dark velvet curtains, flocked red wallpaper, gold leaf Louis XIV chairs, heavy crystal, and ornate flatware, the room was overpowering like the sickening-sweet scent of cheap perfume. A solitary table was set in a bay window.

Candlelight, red wine, and the entire staff had been waiting. As we sat down, I slipped the champagne under the table. An appetizer was instantly placed in front of us, and Bruce orchestrated the conversation like a lawyer interrogating witnesses. Most of the questions were directed to TW.

"What did you think of tonight's production of *A House?*"

"What did you like about Robert's production of *Streetcar?*"

"What would you like to see Robert do next of your plays?"

At times, Robert would join TW in answering a question. I liked him; he was genuine. TW's answers were honest and witty. He was impressed with the young director and told him, "Your *Streetcar* was the best I've seen in many, many years. You understand the poetry, the cadence, and most of all, the characters." Robert beamed. TW laughed loudly.

"I couldn't have done it without the inspiration of your poetic script," Robert graciously replied. TW was very flattered. He laughed louder and longer than usual.

"What of mine will you do next?" TW asked earnestly.

"What would you suggest?"

"I think you would do well with my *Sweet Bird of Youth*. It seems to me, directors rarely get it right. It's about human politics, you know … not love."

"I will have to look into it, Mr. Williams," Robert complied.

We left Biggs at 3:30. A cab was waiting for us outside. I had the warm and shaken bottle of champagne tucked under my arm. TW insisted that I return to his hotel to toast *House*—and we were off.

When we arrived, he nervously tried to tidy up his suite.

"I am sure there is room here somewhere to sit down." He smiled at Scott, signaling him to disappear. "I often get some of my best work done at this time of night."

"Would you like me to leave so you can rest or write?" I asked.

"I thought we might be able to talk, but perhaps these circumstances are not conducive for an honest conversation." He meant Scott was around somewhere. That was my cue to exit stage left.

"I'll call you in the morning," I replied.

"Thank you, baby. That would be best. It was a pleasure having you join me tonight. These events are always very stressful for me. I have some work to do on this production," he said with concern.

"I had a wonderful night. I appreciate your inviting me."

It felt as if I was seeing him for the last time. He looked drained of life. I hugged him. He stood perfectly still. I kissed him on the cheek. He pulled away and sadly looked at me with watery eyes.

"Thank you, baby."

I hugged him again. He stood there rigid. No embrace, no kiss, no affection. "I will talk to you tomorrow." I smiled and moved toward the door.

He stood in the same spot, smiling. "Good night, baby."

I wondered where the passion for life was hiding in him. In temperament, he was so much like the characters he wrote about, but he was emotionally frozen. The dichotomy made no sense to me. He longed for love and affection, but he was unable to give or receive it. He could write about it brilliantly, but he was unable to show it. He told me to take the champagne.

It was 4:30 a.m. when I left. I was exhausted. Outside the Delaware Suites, I uncorked the warm champagne and shook it with my thumb covering the opening, releasing a spray of foamy fluid. I shook until it was empty. It felt good to release the contents.

People worship celebrities like deities. It lifts the spirit to be in the presence of one so sacred. However, celebrities' vulnerabilities are sacrificed on the altar of their fame. Tennessee's soul was drained. He had no refuge in the storm of his famous life. His being lonely and needing a companion made more sense to me now, but I still did not want to play that role. The next day, I called him late in the morning. He had gone back to Key West. Like our first meeting, he remained elusive.

I sent a letter, thanking him for the opportunity to join him at the dress rehearsal of his play. If invited to the premier of *House*, it would be a couple of weeks before I would see him again. Evidently, he came to Chicago during that time but didn't call me. I wondered if there was a rival, but I didn't care. In fact, I hoped he did find someone special to fill the much-needed role of companion in his life. Then I received the second letter ...

Letter #2: It would be nice ...

1432 Duncan St.
Key west, Fla
March 30, '82

Dear Toby:

I was only in Chicago three days, at some depressingly posh hotel along the lake front – the Regency something or other. I didn't leave because of that but because of a very serious piece of miscasting in the play.) Thank God that has now been corrected. The old gent had just had a serious abdominal operation and he suffered a relapse and had to retire from the cast. Well, now, I reckon I'll head back up there soon as the replacement has had a chance to get settled in the part.

These have been troubled days for me. I have a psychophrenic sister who has spent almost half her life in a sanitarium called Stoney Lodge, in Ossinging, N.Y. She became a chain-smoker because of nervous tension, I suppose, developed emphysema and just recently has had to be tranferred to a regular hospital with pneumonia. She's better now, at least temporarily – fever down from 104 to 99. I called her yesterday. She said, 'Hurry up here, Tom, and bring me a carton of Chesterfield cigarettes.*

I'm enquiring about the Miami and Palm Peach area for a sanitarium that will make a more serious effort to control her smoking. If they would only see that she uses a Denicotea holder and changes the filter whenever it gets dark, that provides a good safety measure.

She's the only person in mh family that's very close to me now so I find the situation quite depressing.

When I return to Chicago I hope we'll have a chance to meet often. They've promised to put me in a hotel with a swimming pool this time. Swimming is what keeps me going, I think.

My agent has just informed me that I've been invited to put on a play in Sydney, Australia. If I can find me a good travelling companion I'll attempt it. It's quite a kangaroo hop but they now have a Concorde from London to Singapore that only takes 8 hours. I'm studying maps. I guess with a little island hopping I could make it.

It would be nice to start a new theatre career in such a far away place.

Do you like travel? I've always loved it: been around the world three times and still want more of it.

Yours with love,

Tennessee

(Tom)

Write call your when I'm back
in Chi.

65

Letter #2

1432 Duncan St.

Key West, FL

March 30, 1982

Dear Tony:

I was only in Chicago three days, at some depressingly posh hotel along the lake front—the Regency something-or-other. I didn't leave because of that but because of a very serious piece of miscasting in the play at the Goodman. Thank God that has now been corrected. The old gent had just had a serious abdominal operation, and he suffered a relapse and had to retire from the cast. Well, now, I reckon I'll head back up there soon as the replacement has had a chance to get settled in the part.

These have been troubled days for me. I have a schizo-phrenic sister who has spent almost half her life in a sanitarium called Stony Lodge, in Ossining, N.Y. She became a chain-smoker because of nervous tension, I suppose. She developed emphysema and just recently has had to be transferred to a regular hospital with pneumonia. She's better now, at least temporarily—fever down from 104 to 99. I called her yesterday. She said, "Hurry up here, Tom, and bring me a carton of Chesterfield cigarettes."

I'm inquiring about the Miami and Palm Beach area for a sanitarium that will make a more serious effort to control her smoking. If they would only see that she uses a Denicotea holder and changes the filter whenever it gets dark that provides a good safety measure.

She's the only person in my family that's very close to me now, so I find the situation quite depressing.

When I return to Chicago I hope we'll have a chance to meet often. They've promised to put me in a hotel with a swimming pool this time. Swimming is what keeps me going, I think.

My agent has just informed me that I've been invited to put on a play in Sydney, Australia. If I can find me a good traveling companion, I'll attempt it. It's quite a kangaroo hop, but they now have a Concorde from London to Singapore that only takes eight hours. I'm studying maps. I guess with a little island-hopping I could make it.

It would be nice to start a new theater career in such a faraway place.

Do you like travel? I've always loved it: been around the world three times and still want more of it.

> Yours with love,
> Tennessee (Tom)
> P.S. I will call you when I'm back in Chicago.

Like his first letter, the second was intimate. He was writing me into his life, but I wasn't *living* the adventure with TW. I was still only *watching* it.

CHAPTER 3

THE TRUTH ABOUT SAILORS

CHICAGO: APRIL 1982

I knew he would be returning to Chicago for the premier of *A House Not Meant to Stand*, but I didn't know when. One evening as I arrived home from work, I could hear the phone ringing.

"Hello."

"Hello, baby, how are you?" It was a very exuberant TW, a tone I hadn't heard before.

"Tennessee! It's good to hear from you. When will you be back in town?"

"Yes, yes, call me Tom. After all, that is my real name."

I was flattered. I wondered who else he let call him Tom. I thought it was an indication of his growing interest in thinking of me as his companion. "Okay, Tom."

He chuckled. "I will be in Chicago for the premier of my play tomorrow evening; I would like you to be my guest.

"I would love to join you. Thank you." Excited and concerned about spending time with him, I began to wonder where I was going with these furtive rendezvous.

"I've missed you and hope we can spend time together while I'm there, just the two of us. I'll be in Chicago for a week." His words were spoken tenderly, almost lovingly.

These last-minute invitations added excitement to our time together. It would be flattering to say he was being spontaneous to invite me on the spur of the moment, but I think he simply forgot until the last minute. With plans to meet at the theater around seven, I hung up the phone and realized he genuinely missed me, though it had only been two weeks since I'd last seen him.

The adventure had exceeded my expectations, but it seemed to me we were having different experiences. I was the admiring fan who was awestruck by his genius and loved the adventure. I felt he wanted me to be his companion, perhaps partner. I was entering unchartered waters and wasn't sure how to navigate. Nothing in my life prepared me for what I was experiencing with TW—Tom—the great playwright. I knew I wasn't interested in being his partner; friendship was all I had to offer. Having seen how vulnerable he was, I wanted to be careful not to hurt him. He was accustomed to con men taking advantage of him. I think he saw I wasn't in that category. My interest was to experience him as an artist and, perhaps somewhere along the way, chart my way back to the path of being an artist as well. I would take it a day at a time and be honest about my intentions. That was the best I could do.

The ticket was at the box office, as he'd said. Chicago's elite were invited to the premier of the famous playwright's new work. As cameras flashed like bolts of lightning, the room buzzed in anticipation of this historic night of theater. We hadn't discussed how we would meet, so I asked the first usher I saw.

"Is Tennessee Williams here?" I graciously asked. Tom was beginning to wear off on me.

"Yes, there's a private party for Mr. Williams." Unlike the dress rehearsal, this usher was informed. I took this as a good sign of how the evening would go. He abruptly turned away from me to respond to another guest, but I wasn't done with him.

"Oh, I'm a guest of Mr. Williams. May I enter?"

"We were told not to let anyone enter." He was doing his job. My celebrity status had worn off.

"Were you given the name Tony Narducci as a guest?" I respectfully asked. Maybe there was a special guest list.

"No, we weren't." He was getting irritated.

"I need to get in there!" I persisted. He wanted me to go away, but I had crossed over into interrogation mode. I was not going to sit quietly at the end of the bar this time. "Did he tell you not to let anyone enter?"

"We were told not to let anyone in."

Another usher saw us talking and came to the rescue. He smiled at me. "You are with Mr. Williams."

"Yes, I am." Celebrity revisited.

"I remember you from the dress rehearsal," he said, and then, turning to the other usher, said, "It's okay; he can go in."

I could see Tom at the end of the bar.

He saw me and yelled, "Tony, baby, over here!" Scott looked nervous as I hugged Tom.

"They weren't going to let me in," I said.

Tom looked bewildered. "Why not?"

"They were told not to let anyone in."

Tom turned to Scott.

"Security reasons, I guess," Scott said, avoiding eye contact.

"Well, I'm here now." I smiled at both of them.

"Yes, you are. That's good." Tom recognized that I was being gracious, and he smiled at me. We retreated into the party.

An older woman dressed like a young woman walked up to our table.

"Oh, Mr. Williams, I'm Judith. I've been your biggest fan." A member of Chicago's elite, she was known for her work in the arts. She was directing a photographer to shoot a picture of her with Tom while she prepared Tom for the shot. This was another violation of celebrity, I thought. He was a prop for her vanity. She put her arm around him and pressed her cheek against his as if they were good friends. She was determined to be in Chicago's elite magazines. Tom took it in stride.

"*Streetcar* is the best American play ever written!" she effusively blurted out, all the while directing the photographer where to stand. They were cheek-to-cheek as a smile spread across her face. "Thank you."

Tom graciously smiled as the photographer snapped the shot. Judith quickly pulled away. He looked at me as if to say, "Help me!"

"Thank you, Mr. Williams." She was off to seal another special moment in photography. She never acknowledged me. I was grateful for that.

Greg came up to us. "You can use my office during intermission if you like, or you can greet your adoring public in the lobby. The Goodman is at your feet, Tennessee." Greg smiled and bowed slightly.

"Is it time to go?" Tom was anxious.

"The lights will dim five minutes before Act I begins," Greg reassured him.

Scott took charge. "Thanks, Greg."

People continued to clamor for Tom's attention. He wanted to be protected, so I stayed close to him. "Are you all right?" I asked. He had entered a different zone. Anxiety was driving the moment. His face was flushed scarlet red.

"Oh yes, I'm fine. Opening night always makes me anxious."

"You must have seen many," I acknowledged.

"Oh yes, and I never like to face any of them sober!" We laughed as the lights dimmed. We sat in the same seats we'd had for the preview. This time, I sat next to Tom. I squeezed his hand as Act I began. He ignored my gesture.

He watched as the actors breathed life into his words. This time, there was no conversation between him and the characters on stage. I couldn't read his reaction to this performance. Act I came to an end. There was vigorous applause.

Tom turned to me. He looked frightened, as if danger was all around us. Scott suggested we go to Greg's office to avoid the crowd. We scurried across the theater and walked up the stairs to the manager's office. Greg had arranged a large bowl of iced white wine. Scott opened one and poured us a drink.

Tom guzzled his, as if it were a glass of water. When he finished, he looked up with sad, watery eyes and said, "I don't know what to do." He was focused on his empty glass. The tone was somber, like talking about the death of a loved one. It seemed he was searching for something to erase this moment. Scott poured him another glass of wine, which he swilled like the first. "I can't go back in there," Tom choked out.

"What do you mean?" Scott asked sincerely.

"It's horrible." He turned to look at me. "I think I want to call this off."

As with the rehearsal, I didn't know what to say. I looked at him, hoping the answer would come to me. Even if I had known earlier about the cannibalization of the play, it was too late to do anything about it. Only he had the authority to change it.

"It's not holding together," he said with tears in his eyes. "The actors are just walking through their lines. It's not what I had in mind."

I felt the passion that raged through other works was missing here, but it wasn't as bad as his demeanor and comments indicated. The audience had applauded vigorously. All I could think was that he was depressed, because his reaction—both to the premier and the dress rehearsal—didn't fit the situation.

"Tom, you don't want to do that," Scott quickly replied with genuine concern.

"Yes, I do! I decided against my better judgment to get involved in this production. They have ruined it!" He held his head with both hands. "I thought that replacing the old man would improve everything."

I reached to grab his hand, but he ignored my gesture. I felt his isolation. There seemed to be nothing that would console him. Tears rolled down his cheeks like melting wax. Finally, he turned to me with a tearful smile. "It just isn't ready." It was as if he was at a funeral, overcome with grief. I think he feared this would be the last play he would mount at the Goodman.

I turned to Scott. He was focused on Tom.

"Tom, I think we should go out there and let these people finish their work," Scott said. That was the right thing to say. Scott knew how to keep Tom's mind off disappointment. He was sensitive and decisive in dealing with Tom's moods. I admired his finesse. He knew how to keep him going.

With patience and gentle determination, he got Tom to move. Although he was polite, Scott ignored me. I forgave him his rudeness because I could see he cared about Tom. He was doing what was best for Tom. I believed my presence threatened Scott. I kept a low profile when the three of us were together. Scott had proven he knew how to handle Tom, and I was still clueless.

We avoided the lobby and went right back to our seats. Scott smuggled in a bottle of wine. Act II brought more consternation from Tom. At times, with his head in his hands, he would shake it back and forth and say, "No, no!" Then he'd lift the bottle of wine to his mouth and guzzle it like soda pop on a hot day.

When it was over, Greg escorted us into the bar for a private opening-night party. I moved to the perimeter of the room, so I could get a panoramic view of the swarming, appreciative crowd. Older women came up to Tom to express how grateful they were for a play that touched their lives. Some were more interested in introducing Tom to this person or that person.

Tom became more and more detached. The sad clown smile left his face. He stared beyond the crowd, as if he were focused on something far, far away. Eventually, it was clear he had had enough. He gestured for me to come over. He still looked frightened. I stood close to him, like a protective parent. Vampires continued to swarm, and I wanted to pound a stake into their hearts.

Tom was frantic. "I want to leave. Where's Scott?" he asked in panic mode.

"I'll find him." I scanned the room. Scott was easy to find. His head and shoulders stood out like a lighthouse. I grabbed his arm. "Tom wants to leave."

Scott was instantly at his side. "Tom, I think we should stay a little longer." Scott was the diplomat.

Distress washed over Tom's face. He knew he was the main attraction. He couldn't just disappear. The celebrity has to say good-byes and be appreciative to someone. He had been in this situation before. He knew he was trapped, pinned to a spot like an insect on display.

We stayed a while longer. A woman approached to say how much she appreciated his work and introduced him to her friend. They chatted awhile. He was polite. Eventually, the lights came up, telling us it was time to leave. It was impossible for him to be rude. His gentility and compassion made him hopelessly vulnerable to the ravaging crowd. I could see that he was easy prey.

People slowly left the private party and entered the lobby, where a crowd was still waiting to catch a glimpse of Tennessee Williams. We grabbed our coats and walked out of the Goodman toward Michigan Avenue to find a cab. Scott walked between us.

"Would you like something to eat, Tom?" Scott asked as a cab pulled up.

"Yes, I would." He sounded exhausted and looked as if he had suffered a defeat.

"Where would you like to go?" Scott did his job well.

"Oh, any place is fine. Where would you like to go, Tony?"

"Any place is fine with me too." I deferred to Scott.

"Let's go back to that place where we were with Robert Falls," Tom decided.

"It's late. It may not be open," Scott said.

"Well, let's try it," Tom insisted.

Scott sat in the front seat of the cab, Tom and I in the back. Tom took a deep breath, as if he was trying to fill his lungs with new life. The cool, damp evening fog smelled of seawater. It seemed to calm him. "I feel like a sailor tonight." He was smiling and suddenly in a playful mood.

I admired his ability to quickly recover from disappointment. "How's that?" I asked.

"You know how sometimes late at night, you see three sailors, beautiful young men, looking for excitement and adventure. Sailors always make me think of adventure. I see them on the streets of New York City and wonder what they're up to." Getting farther away from the Goodman improved his mood.

Scott turned around in his seat and looked at Tom quizzically. "Three sailors?" he asked, as if he didn't understand what Tom meant.

"Yes, that's right. Three sailors out on the town, not sure where they're going but filled with anticipation of excitement. That's what we are—three sailors!" He laughed loudly. He was being romantic. I think he wanted to escape the disappointment at the Goodman by creating a new and exciting adventure. We pulled up to Biggs. The interior was dark.

"I'll see if it's open." I jumped out to find the restaurant closed. "Sorry, we're out of luck."

Tom scanned the area and saw lights on in a restaurant up the street, Merewether's. "Let's walk up the block to that place."

We walked up to find it was closed as well. Fog diffused the light, making everything blurred like a dream. We had to walk close to buildings to see if any place was open. There were few people on the street. We were the last three sailors in the world.

"There's got to be something open," Tom insisted. On Rush and State we found a restaurant called Arnie's. It was open, but we were told they'd stopped serving.

A waiter saw us and charged across the room. "It's Tennessee Williams!" he proclaimed to the host, who had just told us we were too late. Thank God for wannabe actors who work as waiters.

"Oh, well, um, follow me," the host said. He didn't know Tennessee Williams from the last customer he'd seated.

The excited waiter escorted us to a center-stage table near a window in the empty restaurant. Tom fell into a chair. The waiter scurried to help him. "I hope this is good for you, Mr. Williams." I sat on Tom's right, Scott on his left. We were sentinels. The waiter was delighted by the late-night serendipity. "What can I get you to drink, Mr. Williams?" He worshiped Tom.

"How about a bottle of your best red wine?" Tom looked as if he would collapse. Suddenly, he turned to Scott. "Oh, I have to take my digestion pills, the green ones." Scott reached into his pocket to extract the needed pills. "Thank you. I need some water."

"Do you want me to get it?" Scott asked.

"No, I need to use the facilities as well." He shuffled toward the men's room.

When Tom was out of sight, Scott turned to me. It was the first time we were alone together. He looked nervous. I wanted him to know I wasn't romantically interested in Tom.

He spoke first. "I've been with Tom for six months now. I love him very much, but we're not lovers. He's been good to me. When I first came to Key West, I didn't know what I was going to do. I had just gotten out of a hospital and needed a place where I wouldn't have a lot of stress. Key West seemed like a good idea." He looked down at the table. Why did he feel compelled to tell me his story? I was impressed at how well he managed Tom through both performances of *House*. That was enough for me to know. Whatever their relationship, it was fine with me.

He went on, "I get depressed easily. Sometimes, I'm so depressed I can't do anything. The doctor said I'm manic-depressive. As long as I'm on medication, I'm okay." I was stunned at how suddenly and candidly he told his story. He didn't seem depressed. He was now looking directly at me. "I've never slept with Tom. I don't think that would be a good idea. It would make me confused. I think it best to just live with him, work for him. He's a very generous man. He helped me recover."

Now that I better understood their relationship, I wanted to reassure him I didn't want his position as caretaker to Tom. "Thank you for telling me that," I said. It took strength to divulge all that to a stranger. Scott was kind and compassionate. I had a great deal of respect for him at that moment.

"I felt you should know what was going on between me and Tom. He likes you very much."

The wine arrived. "May I pour you each a glass?" the waiter politely asked. He held the bottle as if it were a sacred object. A white cotton napkin was wrapped around it. It was more fancy than necessary. Perhaps he was auditioning.

Scott continued. "I think you are a nice person and you treat Tom well. Whatever happens, I will accept it."

I looked at him and leaned into the center of the table. "Scott, I admired how well you helped Tom through the two performances. I felt helpless. I couldn't do what you did." I saw Tom exit the men's room. "And Scott ..." I leaned closer and looked directly at him. "I don't want your job."

Tom was at the table as I finished. "I had the hardest time finding the restroom."

Scott stood up. I thought he was startled by Tom's return. "I need to use it too." He briskly walked off.

Tom looked perplexed. "I think I make him nervous."

"Why's that?"

"Scott never sits still, you know? Whenever I'm around, he's always moving. I get the feeling he doesn't like me." He was serious.

"It looks to me that he cares a lot for you." I had to defend Scott because I knew he had Tom's best interest in mind.

"Well, it doesn't seem that way to me." He looked at me incredulously and guzzled his wine. I hoped he wasn't thinking of firing Scott.

The restaurant had fluorescent lighting, which made everything appear garish. It felt as if we were the characters in Hopper's painting, *Nighthawks*. Although Scott was a devoted companion, I feared Tom was preparing to replace him and looking for a reason to let Scott go. He would be pushing Scott away to make room for me. It would be a mistake. Scott was good for him. But maybe Scott was too passive. It seemed to me Tom wanted a challenge; he wanted what he couldn't have.

"Why don't we go out to dinner tomorrow, just the two of us?" He was smiling at me like a boy who just got a new bike.

"I would love to!" The invitation was exhilarating.

"I don't want Scott around. We haven't spent much time together, just the two of us."

I felt sorry for Scott. Whatever was going on, it was between them. I moved on. "Where would you like to go for dinner?" I asked.

"Wherever, baby."

Scott returned and we ordered. Tom didn't eat his food when it arrived. He said he was too tired. We didn't talk much as we ate. The waiter asked Tom to sign a menu. He graciously scrawled his name across the front of it. Tom left a very generous tip. It was 2:00 a.m.

"I'm tired, baby. I'm going home to bed."

"I think that's a good idea," Scott said. He got a cab and helped Tom into the backseat.

"Call me in the morning, baby," Tom said to me.

"I will, Tom."

Scott held the cab door. He paused before climbing in and turned to look at me. "He'll sleep well tonight. Remember to call him in the morning. Good night." Scott genuinely cared about Tom. I felt I had precipitated the end of his role in our escalating drama.

"Thanks, Scott." The cab disappeared into the fog. I walked to sort out the events of the evening. Dinner alone with Tom; I guessed he wanted to talk about our future. I knew I didn't want to be his live-in companion. From the beginning, I told him I admired him, wanted to learn from him. I never wanted our time together to be more than that. I knew he wanted me in his life. Like Blanche in *Streetcar,* he was wrapping us in illusion. Dinner together would provide the opportunity to put reality in focus.

CHAPTER 4

MORE THAN SHIPS PASSING IN THE NIGHT

CHICAGO: APRIL 28, 1982

I called Tom at 10:00 a.m. to discuss our dinner plan. He was up early, writing, while he eagerly waited for the reviews of *House*. I hoped he would have good news to report when I'd see him this evening.

I arrived early to make sure Tom was ready for our reservation. Now that I was recognized, the doorman let me enter. A light tap on the door, and he quickly opened it. He was wearing a wrinkled, faded gray suit. His tie was askew. A gentleman must be properly dressed for a first date, I thought.

"Hello, baby, come in, come in. It's good to see you." The room was more cluttered than before. His typewriter lay on top of a pile of papers, looking as if it would fall off the tiny side table from which it dangled. I could see a half-typed sheet of paper was held captive in the black lip of the typewriter. He walked over to it to look at what was written. He looked at it as if it were unfamiliar. With a snort, he pulled it out of typewriter bondage, crumpled it in his hands, and threw it to the floor.

"Scott went out. We had an argument over going off to dinner without him." I knew that's how the story would go. I wanted to speak on Scott's behalf, but this issue was between Tom and Scott. Tom was writing Scott out of his life and writing me in. He was agitated. "I have been looking forward to this all day. Some of the reviews were good, particularly Glenna Syse. I think she likes me; she has always given me good reviews. Someday I will have to thank her for her kindness."

Glenna Syse was the best theater critic in Chicago at that time. A good review from her meant more than any other. I wanted to thank her as well. Her review pleased him, which meant dinner would be upbeat, but I wondered what transpired between him and Scott.

Tom walked to the door and motioned for me to exit first. I paused to fix his tie. "Thank you, baby. I'm not sure if I make Scott uncomfortable or if he makes me uncomfortable. Either way, I am pleased that it will be just the two of us."

After last night's earnest and well-intentioned explanation Scott gave me of his relationship with Tom, I felt some responsibility for his welfare. "Do you think Scott will be all right?" I asked.

"Oh, he'll be fine. After all, where is he going to go? He's been living with me for a while. I think he sees this as home."

That was exactly what concerned me. Where would Scott go? Talking about him would complicate the evening, so I let it go. "Tom, would you like to go to my apartment for a drink before dinner? I would like you to meet my roommate."

"Are you lovers?" he asked.

I laughed. It was a question a jealous lover would ask. "No, we're best friends." Danny and I had been roommates for a year since we'd both broken up with our respective partners. We were like brothers. After telling Danny the stories of my adventure with Tom over and over again, I wanted Danny to meet him. He too was a fan.

Tom was smiling ear to ear. Meeting attractive young men always pleased him. "That sounds delightful!" he exclaimed. My apartment was less than ten minutes by car in Chicago's Old Town neighborhood. When we arrived, Tom scanned the apartment complex.

"This reminds me of New Orleans!" The charming, historic landmark Crilly Court Apartments look like the buildings off Bourbon Street. The exterior is red brick with tall, white bay windows jutting out from each apartment. A central courtyard, with white porches and black wrought-iron balconies trimmed with green flower boxes full of red geraniums, added to the charm.

As we entered my apartment, Tom reached into his coat pocket and pulled out a large silver ring with an engraved silver heart dangling from it. "Oh, this damn thing!" He was instantly angry. "After all I've done for the Goodman, I would think they could do better than this!" He threw it to the floor. "Worthless!"

I picked it up to examine it. On one side of the heart, an inscription read *Happy Birthday, Tennessee 3-26-82*. On the other side it read *Your Key to the Goodman's Heart*. It was large, gaudy, and useless. I think it had been in his suit coat pocket since the dress rehearsal birthday party two weeks ago.

"Throw it away; I don't want it," he said with disdain. I think he saw the gift as a sign of their growing lack of interest in his work. Other than the sentimental value, the token was silly, and he felt betrayed. I placed it on the coffee table. I wondered what would make him feel loved by the Goodman.

I could hear Danny in his bedroom, watching TV, so I knocked on his door.

"Could we come in?" We had planned this meeting. I knew Danny was patiently sitting on his bed, waiting for the knock on the door.

"Sure, come on in," Danny replied.

I opened the door and motioned to Tom to enter first. Danny was wearing tight white, Jockey underwear briefs and a white T-shirt. I was surprised he wasn't dressed. He was stretched out on his bed with a pillow propped against the wall that he was leaning on. Danny was twenty-eight years old and in great shape. Tom was pleased and plopped himself down next to Danny on the bed.

"Danny, this is Tennessee Williams." I could see Danny's nervous excitement.

Tom extended his hand to Danny, like a doctor checking a pulse. "Are you ill?" he asked.

Danny leaned forward to shake his hand. He hadn't had a chance to say "pleased to meet you" before Tom asked the question. "No," he chuckled, "I'm just watching TV."

Tom clasped both his hands around Danny's. "Oh, I thought since you were lying in bed, perhaps you were ill." Tom looked at me, wide-eyed, as if to say *He is so good-looking*.

"No, I am just relaxing," Danny said as he blushed.

Tom was still holding Danny's hand. "Why don't you join us for dinner?" he graciously asked.

"Thank you, but I think I am going to relax. I just started a new job, and I need to be on my toes in the morning." Danny lay back on his pillow. He did his best to act naturally while talking to Tennessee Williams in his underwear.

"Perhaps we could do it some other time." Tom was flirting. I realized how compelling Southern charm could be when seducing a young man. Blanche had a good mentor.

Danny smiled nervously. "That would be nice."

"Well, I will be here for the rest of the week. How about one night later in the week?" Tom looked at me as if he needed something. I think he was looking to see if I was jealous of his flirtation.

"I would like that very much." Danny beamed at him.

Tom stood up. "It was a pleasure meeting you. We'll look forward to seeing more of you soon."

I was reminded of *A Streetcar Named Desire* ...

Blanche smiled at how easily she was able to seduce, kiss a beautiful young man, each a distraction from her tired, world-worn body ... each stranger an act of kindness ...

As Tom exited, I turned to Danny and opened my eyes widely as if to say, *so here he is! Isn't it terrific?* He signaled back by widely opening his eyes.

Tom settled on the living room sofa. He clasped his hands behind his head. He looked like a young man who had just had sex for the first time. In a soft voice he said, "You were right; he is a very attractive young man." Tom never missed an opportunity to flirt. His anger over the corny gift was washed away by his encounter with an attractive young man.

We had time before our reservation, so I asked, "Would you like a glass of wine?" There were so many questions I wanted to ask, but we were always on the move in his world.

"Yes, please," Tom replied.

"I'll be right back," I said and darted to the kitchen.

When I returned, he was standing by the small bookcase where I kept early editions of classic literature I had read. He was looking at *Crime and Punishment*.

"I love Russian literature. They have deep souls," he commented as I handed him the glass of wine.

"I would add tortured as well," I added.

"That's what makes them deep. Pain is the essential ingredient of a deep soul." He laughed. "I see you have a nice collection of some very good books." He put Dostoyevsky back on the shelf and returned to the sofa.

"I love classic literature," I said. "That includes great playwrights as well."

He laughed at my inclusion. He had drained the glass of wine by the time he sat on the sofa. "Your roommate is quite attractive."

"Oh yeah, Danny is popular with the boys."

"Why aren't you lovers?" He was genuinely surprised that I could live with an attractive, single young man who wasn't a lover.

"Because we're good friends."

He looked puzzled. "So that makes it even better—good friends and lovers too!" He laughed. I couldn't tell if he was kidding or serious.

"That wouldn't feel right to me."

"Well, have you ever had sex with him?" He had no regard for the conventions most people lived by. There were no boundaries in his world. When the opportunity for sex presented itself, Tom seized it like an eagle snatching prey out of the sky.

"No, we have always been good friends. I couldn't have sex with a good friend. It would feel like having sex with a brother."

He laughed and changed the subject. "What time do we have to leave?"

"Let's go," I said. We were up and moving toward the door. The silver key chain with the big heart dangling from it was on the coffee table where I'd placed it. The Goodman had been good to Tom over the years. Now his work wasn't getting the recognition it once did. The heart key chain was useless, gratuitous, and pretentious. Perhaps it represented defeat to him. I could see why he'd rejected it. Once in the car, his mood quickly changed to sadness. He was crying.

"I think you'll like this restaurant," I said, wanting to keep his mind focused on something light.

But he had something to say. "My mother was a monster, you know, and my father was a drunk and never home." I was surprised at how easily raw emotion seized him. I had read about his troubled relationship with his mother. I think he wanted me to hear his pain from his point of view. Crying was how he was intimate with me. Unfortunately, when he cried, I felt useless. As he continued, he was sobbing. "She was very manipulative, particularly with my sister, Rose. Rose couldn't do anything without Mother's approval. It got so bad that she stopped going out of the house all together. That was when she became very depressed."

His tie was wet with tears. "Rose continued to get more and more withdrawn and then was diagnosed with schizophrenia. Eventually, she had to be put into a hospital. It was horrible!

The doctor told Mother that a simple operation could make her better. She made Rose have one of the first lobotomies performed in this country. It was a cruel, cruel thing to do. Rose was the only member of my family I loved and trusted." He wept as if the incident had just taken place. Although it was years ago, the horror of his mother's act was still raw. "I *never* felt loved by my mother. She is the reason I am all alone. She made it impossible for me to trust anyone, really. I am full of suspicion. I don't think most people are well intentioned." He turned to me for comfort, but I was too inexperienced in life to know what to say, what to do. I reached across the front seat and put my hand on his shoulder.

In Suddenly, Last Summer, *the doctor tells Violet Venable about a new experimental procedure that cuts the depressed, erratic behavior out of a patient's brain, but cautions her that there is no guarantee the operation will be a success; in fact, he warns her it could be fatal. Violet tells him if he wants the money for the new neurological wing of the hospital, he must perform the operation. She insists he must cut into Catherine's brain and remove the salacious lie she is trying to tell about her son, Sebastian.*

"My brother, Dakin, is completely worthless too," he went on. "When I die, I will leave him a dollar. He once gave me streetcar fare. We're not close at all. I have no one." He took out a handkerchief and wiped the tears from his eyes. Although in his seventies, the pain his mother inflicted was still raw like an open wound. I was overwhelmed. We sat in silence the rest of the way to the restaurant.

George's was my favorite bistro at that time. I knew most of the staff who always went out of their way to provide a superb dining experience.

"Dinner for two. The reservation is under Narducci," I said to the maître d'.

"Oh yes, Mr. Narducci, we were looking forward to your dining with us tonight." The host smiled and turned to Tom. "Mr. Williams, it is a pleasure to have you dine with us tonight as well!" The host was very gracious, TW-style.

"Oh, thank you, the pleasure is all mine." Tom laughed. We were seated in the center of the restaurant, but Tom was instantly uncomfortable.

The chosen waiter materialized at our table as we sat. He was young, attractive, and nervous. Thick black hair framed a sharply chiseled face supported by a well-built body full of energy. He couldn't take his eyes off Tom. "Good evening, gentlemen. Welcome to George's." He was looking at Tom like a pet waiting for a command.

"Young man, could you please move us to a booth away from the other tables?" Tom signaled me with a nod of his head in the direction of the young man indicating he thought he was very attractive.

"I am sure that is possible, Mr. Williams. Just let me check with the host." He scurried off to confirm the request.

"He's very good looking," Tom said.

"And eager to please—always a nice combination," I added. We both laughed.

"Perhaps we should invite him to join us afterwards", Tom lasciviously said. Every encounter with an attractive young man was an opportunity for Tom to seduce. There were no filters when it came to lust.

The waiter quickly returned. "That's no problem, Mr. Williams. Please follow me." He led us to a corner table by a wall in a quiet location. "Will this be okay, Mr. Williams?" He helped Tom into the booth.

"Why, thank you. You are a gentleman! Yes, this will be fine." Tom continued to flirt. "Will you still be our waiter?"

"Oh, of course, Mr. Williams." He was trying his best to make everything perfect. Tom was acting like a woman in distress, soaking the moment for every drop of attention.

"Well, I can tell we will be well taken care of." He squeezed the young man's arm. It was a prelude to a kiss. The waiter didn't move until Tom let go.

"What would you like to drink, Mr. Williams?"

"May I see a wine list, please?" The seduction was still in progress.

"Of course, Mr. Williams. I'll be right back." Tom stared at the waiter's ass as he hurried off. He motioned for me to take a look. "I think Chicago likes me." I thought he was referring to the waiter's good service. "The reviews of my play were generally good, particularly Glenna. She understands what the play is about. The one that really bothers me is that Christiansen fellow. I don't think he understands a thing." Richard Christiansen was the other Chicago theater critic. He played second fiddle to Syse, in my opinion.

"Why is that?"

"He compares this play to other plays I've done. I don't know why critics must continually do that! I think that's wrong. My work has matured. I'm not still writing the stories of my youth. This play is about different people, older people. I don't know why critics can't review my work for what it is now. It's worse with the New York critics. I won't go back to New York! They hate me there, you know." He was angry.

I wanted to know more. "They do?"

"Oh yes!" His eyes were watery. "For years, every play I've done there has gotten bad reviews. 'Tennessee is dried up! Williams's work isn't what it used to be!' They're cruel, you know. I won't do another play there." Most of his recent work was criticized for lacking the depth and insight of his earlier work. Tom took every criticism as rejection or insult.

The waiter reappeared with the wine list. "Shall I wait while you look, Mr. Williams?"

"Why yes, that is most considerate of you." Tom signaled me again. The waiter clasped his hands behind him like a young cadet waiting for his assignment. Tom opened the wine list and was quick to order. "We'll have a bottle of the Margaux, please."

"Of course, Mr. Williams." He bowed and went off to get the wine.

"Margaux is my favorite wine, you know. Frankie and I would drink cases of it. It's so delicious."

"So tell me more about the New York critics."

"*Streetcar* and *Menagerie* have always done well, but I'm not a young man anymore. I couldn't write another *Streetcar*. My work now is about older people, people who are different from the early work. *Streetcar* was about young people and what they're concerned with. I don't see why the critics can't review the work on its own merit and stop comparing it to other things I've done before."

The waiter delivered the wine decanted. Tom seized the opportunity to flirt.

"Did you have a glass of our wine, young man?" Tom asked, his tone serious.

The young man was shocked. He didn't get the chide. "Oh no, Mr. Williams! I decanted the wine for you!"

"You did what?" Tom asked, smiling.

"I decanted the wine to open it up, let it breathe." The waiter stood his ground.

"Oh, of course, you decanted the wine." Tom looked at me and winked, still enjoying the flirtation. "I thought you might have had a glass." Tom let out a Big Daddy laugh.

The waiter was struggling to keep up. He didn't understand Tom was flirting. "No, Mr. Williams, I wouldn't do that." Suddenly, he relaxed. On some level, he knew he was being kidded. He carefully poured each of us a glass of wine, wiping the rim of the decanter after each pour with a white linen cloth. We placed our orders and went back to our conversation.

"Perhaps I'll move to Chicago. I have always liked this city. I spent a good amount of time here when I was a young man. Would you work for me if I moved here?"

He caught me off guard. I wanted to hear more about him, the critics, and his work before discussing our relationship. In his mind, I was already his companion. Nothing would stand in the way of his quest. "What about Scott?"

"Things are just not working with Scott. I think I'll have to let him go. I'd like you to work for me. Would you like to do that?"

I hesitated answering. It was too late to help Scott. I felt I'd caused his termination. Did Tom think I wanted to play the role of caretaker/companion? Living with and working for him wouldn't work for me. What about my life? I was a young man, hoping to fulfill my dream of becoming a writer-filmmaker. Tom had already fulfilled his dream. He was looking for a companion to share what was left of his life. I wasn't interested in a serious relationship with anyone at this point in my life. How could I be? I had to figure out my life first, and I had spent enough time with him to know how demanding the job of his companion would be. There would be no time for me to pursue filmmaking. But it was Tennessee Williams, asking for help and support. He'd spent a lifetime dipping into the deep well of emotion in his soul to create sublime works of art that inspired and delighted the world. Now, the well was going dry, and he wanted to be comforted. After a lifetime of giving so much, he deserved to have a loving companion.

It wasn't much to ask, but capitulating represented defeat to me—not so much for giving into what he wanted, but more for giving up what I wanted. I would become consumed in his life. I didn't know how to answer the request. My silence was making him uncomfortable. Maybe there was a way to make this work for both of us. Perhaps discussing it would yield a solution.

"Tom, I'm very flattered that you would ask me to take on that role. How would it work?"

"Oh, I don't need much. Someone to see that I get on and off airplanes, make sure I eat." He paused and laughed. "I sometimes forget to eat, you know."

"Would we need to live together?"

"Yes, I would like that."

I couldn't see how it could work. If I lived with him, I would have to devote a lot of time to managing his life. The amount of time was unknown. If I committed to that, I would have to take his needs into consideration every time I made decisions about my life. He really needed a full-time caretaker like Scott or a companion who would love him and devote his life to him. I couldn't commit to that. And besides, he would have to pay me for my time. I would be a courtesan, taking advantage of an older man, kept in emotional bondage to do his bidding. It would be dishonest. I couldn't live that way.

"Tom, I'm not able to do that right now."

He recoiled, as if I'd stabbed him in the heart with a knife. "You know, I'm lonely. All I want is a little companionship."

I felt his pain. There had to be some way to make this work for both of us. "What you're asking is completely reasonable and mostly, I would love to do it." He was looking at his empty wine glass. "But I need to get back to writing and directing films. I can't give that up. I'm thirty-three years old, and I haven't done anything worthwhile with my life. I want to create something meaningful like you have." I paused, hoping he would say something, but he sat there looking rejected. "How would you feel if we lived with the idea for a while? See how things work out? I would be happy to join you on your engagements and be with you as much as I am able to, but I can't live with you right now. How does that sound?"

He looked up from his empty glass and, with tears in his eyes, came back to the conversation. "Yes, that would be fine." He looked around the room, avoiding eye contact.

"Tom, I wish I could give you exactly what you wanted."

He looked at me and smiled. "I don't want much, you know."

"You deserve everything you want. You have done so many amazing things. Someday, I hope I do a small fraction of what you've done. Life is meaningless otherwise. I have to try."

"I just don't want to be alone. I don't have much time, you know. I don't want to die alone." His eyes were swollen, red, and watery. I'd been honest and direct. What I offered him was truly the best I could do. Anything else would be a deception. I realized at that moment that my hopes for learning how to be an artist from him were foolish. He was completely focused on his own survival. I don't think he could have been accessible to me in the ways I needed. Our salads arrived, and the conversation changed.

"Vanessa wants me to come to Boston this weekend." He furrowed his brow as if to say he was puzzled by this.

"Vanessa?" I had no idea who he was talking about.

"Yes, Vanessa Redgrave. She wants to do a show there with me."

"Boston?" I was completely surprised at how nonchalant he was. Going to Boston to rendezvous with Vanessa Redgrave was like something out of a movie. I was thrilled!

"They fired her from a performance she was to do with the Boston Symphony because of her political views."

"A show?" I had to know every detail.

"Yes, she feels she has been treated unfairly and wants to perform in Boston to protest." Vanessa Redgrave had been hired by the Boston Symphony to recite as they performed

Stravinsky. She was fired because she had expressed sympathy for the Palestinian refugees.

"What kind of show?"

"Oh, I'm not sure. She asked me if I'd read something of mine about being an artist. I wrote a short essay a while ago titled 'An Artist in Revolt,' which I think might be appropriate. She is the greatest living English-speaking actress in the world. She should have the freedom to express her point of view without being judged. People don't understand the difference between the artist and the person." There was fire in his voice. "Would you take me to Boston?" he asked.

I didn't have to live with him to help him meet his commitments. I agreed to go. "I would love to take you to Boston. When would we leave?" How glamorous it will be to work with Tom and Vanessa, two icons of the art and entertainment world. My spirit soared.

"Oh, we'd have to leave sometime this Thursday or Friday."

"I'll figure out a way to take off from work." Spending a weekend with Tennessee Williams and Vanessa Redgrave, as artists in revolt, was heaven compared to the boring tedium of work.

"Good, baby, good." He sounded relieved. "You know, I have new dentures that don't fit. I garble my words. People think I'm always drunk. I must have these fixed if I am to recite."

"Where is your dentist?"

"In Key West. Perhaps he can recommend someone here."
This was something that required time. There was no way he
would have this remedied before the recital.

Dinner had arrived. The Margaux was divine. We easily
finished the first bottle and were on to the second. He was
laughing and telling stories again.

"I love Rome, particularly the Spanish Steps. Frankie and
I went there every summer for many years. My best memories
in life took place there. We were often accompanied by Anna
Magnani, who knew the streets of Rome like a cat. We would
stroll through the most mysterious ancient places I have ever
seen. Anna could talk to anyone. She was able to draw you into
her soul. Not only was she truly Italian, but she was Italy itself! I suggested her face appear on their money!" He laughed
loudly.

I had been to Rome and shared his love for the city. "What
did you like most about Rome?"

"The food!" he blurted out, as if it were obvious. "Eating is
an art for Italians. They love to share stories and life over food.
It's when they are closest. The food is sublime!"

"I love Rome too! Time stands still there. Everything is
fresh and ancient at the same time."

"Tony, I believe you have poetry in you!"

I felt I'd been touched by the hand of God when he said
that. I had to be a filmmaker! I needed this encouragement.

Those words coming from him were like a bolt of lightning from Zeus. A herculean confidence swelled in me. *I am an artist!*

"Perhaps you can take me there some time," he suggested. "We could eat and drink our way up, down, and around the Spanish Steps."

"That would be fabulous, Tom!" This felt good. The place where Fellini drew his inspiration would be an inspiration for me too. Tom would be there as well, to coach me on which scenes were important to capture in our adventure through Rome. We were already making the situation work for both of us without my living with him. We finished our dinner and decided to go to my apartment for cognac. Danny was asleep when we arrived.

We sat on the sofa near where I had placed the key chain.

"How would you like to see Robert Falls's *Streetcar* with me tomorrow afternoon? I think there is a matinee."

"I would love that! I couldn't imagine a better way to see the play than with the playwright."

He laughed. "I will call in the morning and make the arrangements."

We talked about how we would spend the remainder of the week in Chicago before we left for Boston. He would work during the day, and we would have dinner together in the evenings. Things were falling into place nicely.

"Tony, I feel alive, spending time with you. I would be

safe and secure if you were to live with me. Perhaps we could live between Chicago and Key West with occasional trips to Rome? How would that be?"

As wonderful as that sounded, it was his life he was describing. I knew I couldn't be with him all the time. When life is uncertain, it takes experimentation to learn how to get what you want. I knew I had to experiment with making films if I was going to be a filmmaker. That meant going off in search of my destiny. One has to travel light to make the journey a successful one. For now, I would ride the wave of our time together and hope we would be delivered to safe ground. It was midnight when I drove him back to the Delaware Towers.

"Shall we have dinner tomorrow night with your roommate?" He was doing a masterful job of intertwining our lives. I looked forward to spending the rest of the week with him, but I had a gnawing feeling that I would eventually let him down.

"That would be great, and I know Danny would love it."

"Do you mind taking care of reservations again?"

"I'd be happy to." When I pulled up to Delaware Towers, there were tears in his eyes. "Are you all right?" I asked.

"I'll be fine, knowing you will take me to Boston. I fear for Vanessa. She could get hurt doing this sort of thing." He turned to look at me, a smile returning to his face. "Good night, baby. Please call in the morning." He looked exhausted.

"I'll call you at 10:00." I leaned over to kiss his cheek.

He laughed and stepped out of the car. I waited until he was safely in the building. As I drove home, I reflected on the aging genius who had created so many beautiful interpretations of the human experience. He was simply looking for a little comfort before he died. I felt overwhelmed at the thought of taking on that responsibility, but I wanted to help. *A step at a time*, I thought.

The next afternoon, I picked him up at 1:00 for a 2:00 matinee. We sat in the center of the theater in the center row. Robert Falls's *Streetcar* was a beautifully mounted production. The acting, the set, and the direction brought Tennessee's poetry to life. I had only seen the film production of *Streetcar,* but this was a much more moving depiction of the clash between the old refined gentility of Blanche and savage brutality of Stanley.

Seeing a production of *Streetcar* mounted and beautifully performed as the playwright intended was illuminating. I saw so clearly how much of Tom was in *Streetcar.* He was the fragile Blanche, misunderstood and unappreciated by the cruel Stanley—his mother, the world. In the end, her sensitive nature is rescued by a "kind stranger," but ironically, she will live in a psychiatric hospital the rest of her life, alone, unloved. I was the kind stranger he wanted to rescue him, but like Blanche, his rescue was an illusion.

Tom laughed intermittently throughout the production and occasionally had tears in his eyes. This time the laughs and tears were better coordinated with what was taking place on stage. I felt transcendent as I sat there watching Tom watching his work come to life with exquisite precision. I understood the play differently after spending the past few months with him. There were no fallen heroes here—no good guys, no bad guys—instead, there were ordinary people struggling with life, striving for truth, and longing for love. After the play, Robert joined us.

Tom lit up when Robert approached. "It's even better the second time!" he said enthusiastically. Robert had taken good care of Tom's child, and the father was very appreciative. It was the most sincere smile I ever saw on Tom's face. The young director understood him.

Robert smiled appreciatively. "Thank you. I couldn't have done it without your inspired play."

"This truly is one of the better interpretations I have seen in years," Tom said sincerely. Both playwright and director were beaming. I thought it must be rare in theater to have a perfect union of playwright and director.

I wondered if the perfection of this production eased the pain of the fiasco of *A House Not Meant to Stand*.

"You must let me know when you plan to do *Sweet Bird of Youth*," Tom insisted.

"You will be the first to know," Robert said with a smile and genuine sincerity. Tom got up to leave. We shook hands with the gifted director and departed for Delaware Towers.

"I have arranged to move to the Sheraton on Michigan

Avenue," he told me. "There is a swimming pool there that will meet my needs quite nicely. Swimming keeps me alive, you know."

"No problem, Tom. Danny and I will pick you up at 7:30. We'll drive to the Sheraton to check in and then be on our way to dinner."

"Thank you, baby. You're good to me."

I did my best to make him feel taken care of. Without Scott, I didn't know if he would be able to get his daily activities accomplished.

The last couple of days had been magical. I wanted to feel what Tom felt when he saw his work perfectly performed. I wondered if I had the ability to translate life into art. We hadn't discussed my artist vs. businessman dilemma, but seeing him as a successful artist was the inspiration I was looking for. I was eager to get back to the film world. With art and artists is where I belonged.

I made reservations at one of Gordon Sinclair's restaurants, Lexander. Gordon owned two of the best restaurants in the city at that time: Gordon and Lexander. They were next door to each other on Clark Street, between Illinois and Grand. The food in both restaurants was exquisite.

As we drove to the Delaware Towers, Danny was as excited as a kid at Christmas. I knew it would be another interesting night with Tom. When we arrived to pick him up, he was waiting in the lobby, talking to the bellman. I ran in to get him. We were moving him to the Sheraton, and he had left his bags in his suite.

"Good to see you, baby. Do you mind going up to the suite to get my bags?"

"Not at all." I ran up to get them as he continued his conversation with the doorman.

Tom's hotel room was strewn with crumpled-up, partially written-on typing paper. Newspapers were spread out on the couch and table. The TV was on, beds were unmade, and sheets were dragged across the floor, now a familiar sight to me. On a bureau next to his bag, I saw a note from Scott. It was handwritten on a torn piece of paper. Ironically, it was left behind for me to find. The message was short and sweet:

Scott's note to TW

Dear Tom,

Have gone to airport and hope John Murphy has not once again bungled. Hope all goes well on your trip—I think Tony is great. Whatever develops, I trust we can be straightforward.

Much love & best wishes

Scott

P.S. I believe all is packed except papers, medications, phone book, & a couple of things in bathroom.

I knew that my entrance into Tom's life had precipitated Scott's exit. Knowing his struggles with depression and seeing how kind and thoughtful he was with Tom made me feel guilty, though I hadn't done anything to get him fired. I stuffed the note into my coat pocket, picked up Tom's bag, and went back to the lobby. He was smiling when I returned. Once in the car, Tom was the first to speak.

"Why, Danny, it is a pleasure to see you again. Thank you so much for joining us." Tom was a master of grace, a manner that was lost to most people. It was a quality that dated him and distinguished him as well. He made others feel that he was honored to spend time with them. His focus was on making sure others felt special, like Amanda with the gentleman caller in *The Glass Menagerie*. Danny and I were delighted spending time with Tennessee Williams. There was little we could say about ourselves that would compare to the experiences he had.

"Thank you for inviting me," Danny said. I could tell he was nervous. He never imagined in a lifetime he would be having dinner with Tennessee Williams. He gave up the front seat to Tom.

"How was your day, Danny?" Tom asked with genuine interest.

"It was very stressful." Danny was struggling to have a casual conversation with him.

Tom spun his graceful charm. "What do you do to make

a living?" he asked, as if the answer was of great interest to him.

"I am a paralegal," Danny answered with difficulty. He was struggling with the same thing I did that first night. How could Tennessee Williams be interested in the mundane things that we ordinary people do?

"What is that?" Tom sincerely wanted to know.

"I work at a law firm as a legal assistant. I do research to help lawyers prepare for trial, and do other tasks for trials as they come up."

"It sounds very important." Tom laughed as if to say he understood.

Danny didn't know how to read the meaning in the laugh. He looked embarrassed. Tom was merely exercising grace as Amanda Wingfield might, making the evening feel light and carefree, seemingly interested in knowing everything about the guest. Danny quickly recovered. "Tony said your new play is very good."

"I suppose some have liked it; others haven't."

"Are you working on anything now?" Danny was relaxing into being with Tom.

"Oh yes, I am always working on something."

Danny was stumped. He had taken the conversation as far as he could. When we arrived at the Sheraton, I left the car with the valet. We went to check Tom in, and then we took the elevator up to his room. The first thing he did when we entered was to open his typewriter case and place the portal to his soul on the desk, ready for use. The rest of the luggage could wait to be opened later. When we got back to the car, Tom realized he'd forgotten his medication.

He turned to me and asked, "Darling, do you mind going up to get my pills—two of the green ones and one of the tiny white ones?"

"Sure, I'll be right back." Fortunately, I knew which pills he was referring to, so I was back in five minutes, and we were on our way.

"Thank you, baby." Tom was becoming more and more affectionate in how he talked with me. For the rest of our time together, he called me baby.

We arrived early for our reservation. Gordon had a table waiting for us on the second level in a private corner, away from the crowd. Gordon fussed over us to make sure everything was perfect, and it was. Tom was in good spirits. He was happy to be dining with two young men who were completely focused on ensuring he had a good time, and he dominated most of the conversation. That was good with me and Danny.

"My pancreas isn't functioning well. I have to take all sorts of medication to stay alive." He laughed loudly, looking at Danny. He talked on about his failing health and the plethora of pills he had to remember to take for different maladies. He went on to talk about his loose dentures and his fear of losing them in the middle of a sentence. Danny was soaking up every word of the kind hearted gentleman. Tom drained several glasses of sauvignon blanc. Gordon joined us toward the end of our evening to pay his respects to the honored guest and buy us cognacs. After three hours of dining and drinking, Tom said he was tired.

We drove him back to the Sheraton. This evening was the most animated I had seen Tom. Being with young men amplified his spirit. He exited the car, smiling and laughing. I made sure he got to his door and assured him I would call in the morning.

Back in the car, Danny was glowing from a night spent with the great literary genius. We chatted all the way home about how entertaining Tom was.

"He is so down to earth," Danny said with surprise.

"I know. It was hard for me to let him be human. I want him to be a god," I said with a chuckle. But I wanted Danny's reaction to what he observed about me and Tom. Danny was smart and insightful. "So what do you think?"

"What do you mean?" he asked.

"Does it look like he and I are friends or something more than friends?"

Danny took his time to answer. "I don't know. All I saw was a nice, gentile man. I couldn't read anything else."

I wanted him to say more. "I think he is in love with me," I said abruptly.

"I didn't see any of that," Danny chuckled.

I needed someone to help me figure things out. "Last night at dinner, he asked me to move in with him, be his companion, and help him manage his life. There's no road map for what to do when an aging genius asks a career-challenged young man to be his companion. I don't know what to do."

"Could you do that?" Danny asked incredulously.

"My gut says no, but I feel some responsibility for this great man's welfare. It's as if fate asked me what is more important in my life: what I want for me or what Tennessee Williams wants me to do for him."

"Wow, I have no idea what to tell you," Danny said honestly.

"If he was my age and struggling to be the playwright he would become, it would be perfect. He would write the words; I would turn them into films."

"So it's the age difference?" Danny asked.

"Yes, partially, but more important, it's the difference in our stages in life. He accomplished his dream. I'm still asleep, and my dream hasn't begun yet."

"But it's Tennessee Williams," Danny flippantly interjected.

"I know, I know." There was nothing anyone could tell me about how this should go. I was on my own.

"Maybe he could help you get into film? He must know a lot of important directors and actors."

The thought had crossed my mind on several occasions,

but I was reluctant to ask for a favor. That would make me more obligated to him. I didn't want my life to get inextricably intertwined with his. The more I thought about it, the more confused I became. "I've thought of that, but I fear he would want something I couldn't give him in return."

"What is that?" Danny asked.

"My love, my life."

We sat in silence the rest of the way home. As we pulled up to our apartment, Danny said, "I don't know what to tell you." He was right. No one could tell me what was best to do. I would have to figure that out on my own. It was the last time Danny would see him.

A couple of nights later, I made reservations at a popular Chinese restaurant called Susie Wong's. It was known for having good food and an excellent piano bar. I invited a few friends who were eager to meet Tom to join us.

We arrived late to find we were seated in the middle of the crowded restaurant at a large round table. Tom was uncomfortable sitting in the center of the room. I thought perhaps a table full of attractive, articulate young men would insulate him from the crowd, but his mood was somber.

The boys' conversation was about everything other than Tennessee Williams: jobs, parties, gossip, clothes. Tom shared little of himself with them. His comments were brief and general, very different from dinner with Danny. Later, I came to realize that Tom was quiet because the people were pretentious. Their boasting about careers and mentioning famous people they knew made Tom uncomfortable. I think they thought it would impress him. He preferred the humble, more gentile conversation he'd had with Danny. In time, those people would be out of my life, and my friendship with Danny would become richer and fuller.

For the entire evening the piano player was singing Cole Porter, George Gershwin, and other classic composers of that time. When it came time to leave, Tom asked if we could stay and sit around the piano. We sat in the last two available seats, not next to each other.

I had been going to piano bars for years. I loved listening to talented, unknown people sing old ballads. Having an after-dinner drink with Tennessee Williams and Cole Porter was magical for me. The piano player was singing *Night and Day*. Tom sang along. The next song was *Just One of Those Things*. Tom struggled through singing it and eventually gave up to the agile piano player. When the song was finished, Tom asked, "Do you know *Danny Boy*?"

"Why, of course I do. Would you like me to play it?"

"Yes, I would appreciate it very much, and I would like to sing it myself!" He laughed, and the cheerful piano player slowly began to play it. The small group assembled around the piano was silent and focused on him. At the appropriate time, Tom stood up and began to sing. His voice was weak and he slurred the words, but with passion and tears in his eyes, he became the song ...

> *Oh Danny boy, the pipes, the pipes are calling*
> *From glen to glen, and down the mountainside*
> *The summer's gone, and all the flowers are dying*
> *'Tis you, 'tis you must go and I must bide.*
> *But come ye back when summer's in the meadow*
> *Or when the valley's hushed and white with snow*
> *'Tis I'll be here in sunshine or in shadow*
> *Oh Danny boy, oh Danny boy, I love you so ...*

He looked at me the entire time he sang. Was I his Danny Boy? When he was done, he sat down and took out a handkerchief to wipe the tears from his eyes. Everyone applauded vigorously. I gazed in awe at the spontaneous emotion that poured out of him and at the courage it took to stand and sing his heart out. At that moment, I could see where the power to express the joy and pain of being human came from. He looked up from his handkerchief and said to me, "I think it's time to go."

"Okay." I smiled back.

Tom went around the table to shake hands with the piano player and thank him for giving him the opportunity to sing one of his favorite songs. The piano player stood up and said, "The pleasure was all mine. You sang beautifully!" Tom laughed and with humility, thanked him again. He was kind and charming to the small group who had shared this moment with him. I didn't know if they knew who he was, and it didn't matter. Slowly, we moved toward the exit. I told him to wait and I would get the car to pick him up. On the way back to the Sheraton a quiet tranquility came over him.

"I love that song. It reminds me of my youth," he said with nostalgia in his voice. I had never really listened to the words before tonight. The lyrics captured his life, his loves, and the multitude of loss he endured. Perhaps it reminded him of Frankie. When we arrived at the Sheraton, he turned to look at me. "I have a busy day tomorrow. I'll have to make arrangements for our trip to Boston this weekend. Call me in the morning, baby." There were silent tears in his eyes. I reached across the front seat to embrace him. He was stiff and unresponsive, but it felt good to hug him. I watched him enter the building and turn to walk to the elevators.

CHAPTER 5

ARTISTS IN REVOLT!

BOSTON: APRIL 30, 1982

I picked up Tom on Friday afternoon for our flight to Boston. He was waiting in the lobby, chatting with the doorman about how much he loved swimming. He was wearing the same wrinkled gray suit with the necktie askew. I hugged him and straightened his tie. He was cheerful and looked well rested. The swollen red eyes were at rest. A rolled up piece of paper was in his right hand. I hoped it was our itinerary.

"Good to see you, baby. Do you mind carrying my bag?"

"Not at all." Since we would be in Boston for just the weekend, I didn't have to make up a story to take off work, but I would have done anything to witness this historic event. I was bursting with excitement—Tom, Vanessa, and me. "Are you ready, Tom?"

"Yes, baby." We got into my car and we sped off to O'Hare. "I wasn't able to get hold of Vanessa. I hope she knows I'm coming." We were off on our quest without confirmation that it would occur. I was anxious for him.

"Where are we staying?" I asked in hopes he knew.

"The Ritz-Carlton. We have two rooms, one for each of us. Vanessa told me a while back that she would make all the arrangements and will be staying there as well."

"When did you last speak with her?" I wanted to be as useful as I could be. If I knew all the details, I could ensure things went smoothly.

He was lucid and cheerful. "She recently called me in Key West."

"So you're sure she'll be there?"

He was getting uncomfortable with my questioning. "I don't know, baby. I suppose she will. It is her show." He looked at me and laughed. It was his way of saying *Don't worry*. We were riding the wind and sea. Two sailors bound for Boston with an uncharted adventure ahead of us, but the pilot said it would be all right.

Tom sat in back of me in first class, next to a young man with whom he chatted the entire way. He laughed, spoke loudly, and drank plenty of white wine. The young man was entertained, and Tom got to flirt. He found out that the young man had a car at the airport. When we landed, Tom asked if he would give us a ride to the Ritz. The clueless young man happily agreed.

Tom sat in the front seat. He charmed our chauffeur with

more questions and compliments. Watching the seduction intrigued me. Affability and grace reeled the boy in. When we arrived, he quickly jumped out of the car to retrieve our bags, enthusiastically shook our hands, and said, "Pleasure meeting you."

"Thank you so much for the ride. You are a gentleman." Tom laughed and turned to enter the hotel. I said good-bye to our brief companion. I don't think he knew that the gregarious older man who had "picked him up" was Tennessee Williams.

We checked into the Ritz and learned Vanessa was already registered. Things magically fell into place for Tom. I had to learn to trust the winds that always took us sailors to a safe port. A good sailor was never lost.

I quickly unpacked and went to his room. The TV was on, and a newscaster was reporting on the Boston Symphony's firing of Vanessa Redgrave. There she was, telling a reporter how being fired by the BSO was unfair and she didn't want people to confuse her artistry with her politics. She was here to show them the difference. Tom looked at the TV and then at me.

"I hope she doesn't get hurt doing this." He looked concerned.

As an artist in revolt, I was surprised at his fear. "What do you mean?"

"Boston is not all that civilized. One doesn't know what to expect here, you know." He moved around the room, emptying his bag and hanging clothes. "Vanessa may be an unparalleled actress, but that won't protect her from danger." He looked at me. I could see distress in his face. I think he feared she could be killed. I didn't read danger in what the TV was broadcasting or in what Vanessa was doing to deal with the situation. I thought he was projecting his fear on to her. "Is it okay to be here, baby?"

Did he mean was I okay, being here with him, or were we in danger by doing this with Vanessa? "Yes, of course, it's exciting! It will all be fine," I reassured him that there was nothing to fear, but it was his nature to worry. He looked like a frightened child. The degree of concern was greater than the situation warranted. I wondered how many times as a child he'd sat in fear, his parents unable or unwilling to recognize and respond to the unique sensitivities of their gifted son. "Good, good," he said as the phone rang. It was Vanessa, letting us know that she would be tied up all evening but would call in the morning to make arrangements. How was this going to come together? Who would do what and when? The businessman in me wanted to have a plan.

"Tom, do you have a copy of the essay you're going to read?" That question popped in my head all of a sudden because, as a business man, I knew what it was like to show up for an important meeting without the materials needed to conduct the meeting.

"No, but I'm sure we can find one in Boston somewhere.

After all, this is the city of higher learning." He laughed and shrugged it off as if he knew, without knowing, that it would all come together. The winds were blowing again, and this time Tom wouldn't be the pilot; I knew I would have to play that role.

I was mystified that he had no idea where the book would come from. So, I began my investigation to track it down. "What's the title of the book?"

"Oh, I think its *Collected Essays* or *Complete Essays*— something like that. It's Grove Press."

What if I couldn't find it? What if it was out of print? How could he read without a copy of the essay? "Tom, what if we don't find the book?" Why was I worried if he wasn't? I was becoming the caretaker. The circumstances were grooming me for that role.

"I don't know, baby. Maybe Harvard would have my book. I think they like me there," he chuckled. "We'll call in the morning."

It was late. We ordered a bottle of white wine and cold roast beef sandwiches. It was all the kitchen had to offer. I gobbled the sandwich down and drank most of the wine before retiring to my room.

The next morning I was awakened by a phone call from Tom, asking me to come to his room. I got out of bed and opened the curtains. The morning sun burst in like the arrival of a deity. I could see swatches of green grass peeking through the gray carpet of winter, pearls of white blossoms on trees, and red, yellow, and blue tulips heralding the spring. A sapphire blue sky framed the landscape. It was a beautiful day.

I was at Tom's door within fifteen minutes. I knocked and entered to find him sitting in the bay window in a white cotton robe, reading the *Boston Globe*. He was bathed in light and looked like a prophet in a Renaissance painting.

"Oh, Tony, good morning." I bent over to kiss him on the cheek. He looked surprised, as if seeing me for the first time. Simple affection was strange to him. "Thank you, baby. Vanessa made the morning papers. It explains here why she was fired and what she plans to do as a result. We're not mentioned in the program. She called to say she'd be busy all morning but will meet us for lunch." Although I knew she was checked into the hotel, she was still elusive.

"Would you like me to order breakfast?" I was hungry.

"I've eaten, but why don't you call room service and order something."

I ordered a croissant, freshly squeezed grapefruit juice, and coffee.

"You know, we must find a typewriter. I'll need one to work this afternoon." A typewriter was an essential appendage wherever he was.

"Where can we get one?" Again I was being practical.

"Call the front desk and ask." Of course, he had been in

this situation many times before and knew exactly what to do.

I quickly tracked down a typewriter, to be delivered by noon. My breakfast arrived and Tom joined me for a cup of coffee.

"It's a beautiful day, baby. You should go for a walk. I'd like to do some writing, you know."

"That's fine. I have a friend who works near here. I'd like to see him."

"Good, good."

"Will you be okay while I am gone?" I was concerned for his welfare. I surprised myself at how easily I wore the role of companion/manager.

"I should be. I think the Ritz will be able to accommodate my needs."

"I'll call before I return. Anything I can get you now?" Even being caretaker was becoming more natural.

"You know, I don't like being left alone. I get frightened. Several years ago, after Frankie died, I was kidnapped. I don't know who it was. The police never found out. The kidnappers wanted me to write a manuscript under a pseudonym. I thought they were going to kill me if I didn't produce something. But I couldn't write because I was so frightened."

I never read about a kidnapping, but I was fascinated. "What happened?"

"They tied me up, you know. How could I write tied up?

Eventually, they untied me, and I managed to get some words down. I have never been so scared. What were they thinking? A Tennessee Williams script would get them millions in ransom? Who would pay that much for a playwright?" He laughed.

"What did you do?" I asked, eager to hear how it ended.

"I couldn't write. They threatened me and that made me more frightened. My hands were shaking so much that I couldn't hit the right keys on the typewriter! It felt as if I was there for days. I really don't know how long it was. They didn't want to kill me, and they couldn't get me to write, so they let me go."

"How did they let you go?"

"Oh, they blindfolded me just as they had when they abducted me and threw me in the backseat of a car. Next thing I knew, I was sitting on a beach, not far from my home."

"Were they caught?"

"No. The police had no leads, and there wasn't any evidence."

What a great story! He could have turned the experience into a play, I thought—but I wondered if the story was true. If it was, it helped to explain his fear for Vanessa.

He changed the subject. "You know, I've met mostly con men my entire life. They all want something, and they think I can give it to them." His eyes welled up with tears, and he began to chuckle. He cried as often and as easily as a baby. Con men were a theme throughout our time together. I wasn't sure if he kept bringing it up to get reassurance I wasn't one or if he wanted me to protect him from the deception to which he was easily vulnerable. "Oh, I'm crying." He laughed out loud. "It seems I cry more easily the older I get." He turned and looked at me intently. "I'm tired of con men. I need someone who cares for me. You know, I don't have much time left."

As before, I didn't know what to say. I knew he was lonely and frightened. I believe he wanted me to assure him that I would be with him forever. I couldn't deceive him with promises I knew I couldn't keep. A smile was all I could provide. The words he needed to hear would not form in my mouth.

"Tom, why do you believe you don't have much time left?" We'd had this conversation before.

"You know very little works well in my body. I need to take pills for my inactive pancreas, pills to help me digest my food, pills to calm my nerves. I've been an insomniac since I was eight years old, and I get up every couple of hours and take Seconal to get back to sleep. Maybe I stay alive because of all these chemicals." He laughed loudly as he dried his eyes with the sleeve of his robe. "They say I'm a drug addict—at least my brother, Dakin, thinks so. I'm not very fond of him. He is critical, like my mother. I need these pills to stay alive, you know."

I passed no judgment on his use of pills. As a boy, I watched my mother pop pills all day. She had high blood pressure, pleurisy, weight problems, and diabetes. Taking pills to stay alive was a way of life for her. I believed that was true for him as well. He gulped his coffee, and I finished my breakfast.

"Well, I'm going to work now, baby." He looked peaceful.

"Okay, I'll call you about noon to see about lunch."

"Good, good." He returned to his newspaper. The sunlight had intensified around him. His hair looked repelled by his head. Strands of it stuck out like beams of light from a halo. I thought he would levitate.

I walked across the Public Garden toward downtown Boston. The park was filled with people, strolling, sunbathing, hustling money, or selling cheap merchandise. A group of elderly citizens slowly escorted a parade of preschoolers across the Common. Everything the children saw produced a barrage of questions. Every question got a detailed answer from the elderly that couldn't hold the attention of the children. It made me think: life begins in oblivion and ends with talking too much.

Eventually, I got to Houghton Mifflin, where my friend Chris Johnson was working as an editor. Chris and I met in 1974 when we were newly hired English teachers at Downers Grove North High School. We quickly became friends because of our mutual interest in film and literature.

Coincidentally, Chris's wife, Barb, and I met at Northern Illinois University in the late 1960s. Chris, Barb, and I would spend many nights drinking copious amounts of Scotch, smoking packs of cigarettes, and solving the problems of the world. We were children of the 1960s who loved exercising our minds on the meaning of everything and the problems with all of it.

I called Tom at noon.

"We're to meet Vanessa at 2:00 in the lobby," he told me.

"I'll be in your room at 1:30," I said enthusiastically, knowing I would meet Vanessa Redgrave.

"Good, good." He sounded upbeat.

As I began to walk back to the Ritz, I became haunted by the elusive essay. Anxious, but determined, I would find it. I returned to the hotel and put on a suit. I knew Tom would be in a suit. He was not in his room when I arrived, but there was a note telling me he had stepped out to buy a necktie and to meet him in the lobby bar. I went down to wait for him. He arrived with a new tie slightly askew, and I straightened it.

"Thank you, baby. How was your day?"

"Good. I met up with a friend I haven't seen in a while, someone I'd like you to meet."

"Is he good-looking?" It was another opportunity for him to exercise his libido.

"He's attractive. What about Vanessa?" I knew he looked forward to seeing her. I didn't want to get into the conversation about whether or not I'd slept with Chris.

"I left a message for her to meet us in the Montgomery Bar."

We sat in a corner by a window, where we could see the carnival of people strolling through the Public Garden. A waiter dressed like Fred Astaire in *Top Hat* came up to our table. "Would you care for a drink?" His demeanor was very formal. He spoke very articulately, as if addressing a queen. (No pun intended.)

"Yes, a white wine, please. Baby, what would you like?"

"I'll have a white wine too, please."

The waiter bowed, turned, and tap danced to the bar. Across the room, two middle-aged women wearing 1940s-style hats and gloves were having a serious conversation over lunch. Next to them, a group of businessmen talked loudly and took notes. They looked like a commercial for an insurance company. The walls of the bar were dark mahogany. Tables with white linen tablecloths speckled the room. The setting was perfect for a conversation with Tennessee Williams.

"How was your day?" I started.

"Good, good. I did some writing and took a long nap." He smiled as he looked out the window. "This good weather brings out many attractive young men. Did you see many on your walk?"

"Yes, many," I said, as if sharing gossip with a friend.

"And did you meet any?" His tone was like a lover hearing about an infidelity.

"No, I went to see my friend Chris."

He turned from the window and looked at me quizzically. "Do you sleep with Chris?"

I laughed. I knew we would have this conversation. After a while, I couldn't tell if he was jealous or just enjoyed talking about sex. "No, he's straight, and besides, he's happily married to my friend Barb."

He shrugged it off. "I think everyone should be as sensual as possible. Perhaps I can sleep with your friend Chris!" He laughed out loud at his boldness.

I played along with him. "Perhaps I can arrange it."

He liked sparring. "Yes, that would be nice." We both laughed. "You know, when Frankie and I traveled, we would meet many different, attractive young men. Sometimes one of us would go home with one of them. It was a competition between me and Frankie to see who could attract the most men. He won most of the time. He knew how to flirt, and he was good-looking. It was rather harmless, you know. From time to time, Frankie would carry on too long with one of them, and I would get jealous. I think it was a game we played. He wanted me to get jealous. Then we'd make up. I always forgave him, you know. I loved Frankie very much. He was the love of my life." He became choked up. "But you know"—he paused to gulp his wine—"Frankie *never* told me he loved me." He looked at me with a sad Kabuki face. Tears rolled down his cheeks as he remembered the absence of those three words from Frankie.

"He didn't?" I was astonished he'd never heard the words "I love you" from him. How could he call Frankie the love of his life and refer to that time as the happiest of his life, not knowing if he was loved in return? If that were true, then he never knew he was loved. His mother was a "monster." His father was absent and a drunk. His brother was incapable of relating to him, and his sister, Rose, was institutionalized with schizophrenia and dependent on him. He didn't feel loved by the people whom he loved the most. Perhaps this was the source of his fear, his despair. His life was slipping away, and he feared it would end, feeling he had never been loved.

Constantly wanting to know with whom I slept was a game he started as a competition with Frankie, the man he called the love of his life. He and Frankie had no boundaries. Anything was fair game. That meant he always felt vulnerable. I was overcome with compassion for him.

"No, Frankie never told me he loved me!" There was defiance in his voice. "I think he didn't say it to me so that he would have something over me." That meant Frankie always kept him on the defensive, making Tom "beg" for love. He dried his eyes with his napkin. His tone changed to pride. "He was a little jealous of me too, you know." He leaned forward as if to tell a secret. "He complained that people liked him only because he was with me. He didn't feel he could do anything on his own."

Frankie sounded more like a wife than a partner. "What did he do for a living?" I asked.

Tom was puzzled. He looked down and thought for a moment. "He was my lover, and he loved opera." He laughed.

So, Frankie was a kept man. Tom supported him through their entire relationship. I wondered what Frankie contributed to their time together. "He played opera all the time, especially the early operas of Maria Callas. Frankie had them all. He loved music. I think all Italians do. Do you?" he asked.

"Yes, I love opera very much, especially the early recordings of Maria Callas." I was astonished at the similarities between me and Frankie. We were both Sicilian, we worshiped Maria Callas, and we were objects of Tennessee Williams's desire. However, I worked my entire life to take care of myself, and I wasn't a con man. Frankie fed off Tom's fame and generosity, and Tom let him do it.

"Yes, good, good. You're very much like Frankie, you know. You're built like him, and you love opera." He paused to gulp his wine.

I didn't like being compared to Frankie anymore. I wondered if Frankie was the original con man. Everything I'd heard led me to believe it was true. Frankie didn't work; Tom supported him. Frankie openly had affairs, which Tom overlooked because he felt lucky to be with an attractive, sexy Italian. Worst of all, he kept Tom dangling on a string by never saying "I love you" to him. Was Frankie's withholding those words the reason for Tom's distrust of men and was his mother's lack of loving him the source of his not feeling worthy of being loved, or recognizing love when presented to him? His relationship with Frankie wasn't a blueprint for happiness. At times, Tom played the fool—or was it codependence that kept them together, hopelessly addicted to dysfunctional relationships? Because he couldn't bring himself to admit that (who could), he condemned the very type of man, the con man, to whom he was hopelessly vulnerable. Unfortunately, he was still surrounded by con men. Of course, this was all speculation on my part, but it made sense.

I was the redesigned version of Frankie, without the codependence and the usury. He wanted to hear the words "I love you" from me to fill the hole Frankie left in his soul. Ironically, I wasn't in love with him either and couldn't say those words as well. I'm not a psychologist, only a student of literature, but literature has taught me how to read the human soul, especially the work of Tennessee Williams.

"We were very sensual, you know. Frankie loved sex. He wanted to have sex all the time. He would wear me out. Do you like sex that much?" So Frankie was a sex addict too.

"Yes, very much."

He scrutinized me. "Yes, I can tell you do. You're very sensual. Italians are very sensual. Do you have sex often?"

"Often enough," I replied.

He laughed, as if I'd told a joke. "Good. You should have

it as often as possible. But the 'gay plague' worries me." He gulped his wine.

"Yes, it worries me too."

"Gay men have so much more freedom now than when I was a young man. It's easy to see how it could quickly spread with the rampant promiscuity most young gay men indulge in these days. Always use condoms." He was looking directly at me. "I wonder where Vanessa is." The Astaire waiter came up to our table to tell Tom there was a call for him. "Where do I go?"

"I can bring a phone to you, if you'd like?"

"Yes, that would be good." The waiter returned with a phone. It was Vanessa, magically on cue. It was a brief conversation.

"We're to meet her on the mezzanine to have lunch," Tom informed me. "She'll be there shortly." We left the bar and walked up the stairs to the mezzanine. It was midafternoon, and no one was there. The restaurant staff must have been told that the two celebs were coming for a private lunch. A large round table was set up in the middle of the room with their finest crystal and flatware.

A smiling waiter promptly walked up to us. "Drinks, gentlemen?"

"Yes, a white wine for me. Tony?"

"White wine, please."

Tom was anxious, as if he were meeting Vanessa for the

first time. "Where's Vanessa?" He looked around the empty room. There was no sign of Vanessa, simply because we had arrived before her. "Do you suppose we're in the right restaurant?" he asked.

"This is the only mezzanine in the hotel." From where I was sitting, I could see the elevator doors open. A well-built, official-looking black man exited and came toward us.

"Mr. Williams?"

I thought he was with the FBI—no expression on his face, no variance in his voice, disciplined in his approach. He was young and looked like a fashion model—perfectly groomed and wearing a brown sport coat, no tie, and tight pants.

"Yes." Tom flashed a smile and looked at me, signaling he found the officious young man attractive.

"Ms. Redgrave will be down shortly. My name is Randolph. I'm traveling with Ms. Redgrave. Do you mind if I join you?" So was he her bodyguard? My first thought was that she was having an affair with this picture-perfect guy. I quickly realized I was beginning to think like Tom.

"Oh no, please do!" Tom shrugged his shoulders and looked quite pleased. "And what do you do for Ms. Redgrave?" Tom's tone turned to seduction.

"I make sure things are taken care of." He looked around the room and then positioned himself in a chair where he could see the stairs and the elevator. He definitely was her bodyguard. I wondered if she always traveled with a bodyguard, or was she, like Tom, concerned for her safety while in Boston? In either case, I felt safer having Randolph around, watching the elevators and the exits. A waiter came up to deliver our drinks and asked Randolph if he wanted one.

"No, thank you," he said with a straight face and then looked around the room again. He couldn't drink while on the job. The elevator doors opened and a group of people stepped out, among them Vanessa. Wearing a simple light-blue dress, she lit up the room. She was the last to exit. Ahead of her were another official-looking man and a strikingly good-looking younger man, with whom she was conversing. They walked up to the table from behind Tom. Vanessa wrapped her arms around him.

"Hello, Tennessee!" She looked very pleased to see him. Tom attempted to stand while Vanessa hugged him. They embraced tenderly.

"Vanessa, it's good to see you, darling!"

She kissed him on the cheek. I stood up and smiled in her direction. She caught my smile. "Hello, Tony." She knew my name. What a pro! I was flattered. The group gathered around the table. Phillip, the young man, sat on Vanessa's right, Randolph on her left. Vanessa introduced everyone. Tom stood as Vanessa began introductions. "Tennessee, Tony, this is Phillip and Randolph." Phillip was an actor who would be performing with her. I wondered what roles he played and how she'd selected him. He was lucky to be the chosen one to perform with her. Smiles flashed across the table. Still standing, Tom was beaming down at Vanessa like a good father. He was a perfect gentleman, waiting for the lady to be comfortably seated before he sat. "Please sit, Tennessee," Vanessa said, graciously acknowledging his gentlemanly behavior.

"Thank you." He sat, smiling in her direction.

"Sorry to keep you waiting, but I've had endless meetings since we've arrived."

"Oh, no problem. Tony and I have been keeping ourselves amused."

I smiled nervously, suddenly becoming very self-conscious about how Vanessa saw me. Did she think I was a friend, lover, his caretaker, manager, or a traveling companion? I listened carefully for an opportunity to say something intelligent to contribute to the conversation. Tom and Vanessa exchanged pleasantries. I was getting anxious, sitting in my blue-gray Armani suit, smiling like a good listener but silent, like a dolt.

"I hope it's been pleasant for you being here, Tennessee."

"Oh yes, darling. Our accommodations are very nice."

"Good, I'm pleased to hear that." Vanessa was friendly and genuine. I began to look at her closely. She wasn't wearing makeup. Her skin was translucent. Her azure-blue eyes caught the light and sparkled like sapphires. Short-cropped reddish hair, casually combed back, framed a perfectly shaped face. She was beautiful.

"We saw you on TV," Tom said.

"Oh?" Vanessa leaned toward Tom.

He looked worried. "Yes. You were being interviewed about your contract with the Boston Symphony."

"Oh yes. That's where we were this morning."

I recalled Vanessa in the film *Isadora*. Like Isadora Duncan, Vanessa was fighting for freedom of expression. Tonight, she would dance and recite her point of view on the sanctity of art.

Tom looked anxious. "Are you all right, darling?" he asked her. He was more concerned that she wouldn't be harmed than he was in preparing for her show. He didn't have his essay, nor did he know where to get it, and he hadn't rehearsed, but none of that was as important as Vanessa's safety.

"Oh yes, marvelous. Although we've been quite busy, I think everything is in order for this evening."

"Good, good. I think I'll read my essay 'An Artist in Revolt.'" I was surprised that he hadn't discussed this with her in advance.

"That sounds lovely, Tennessee. Phillip will be working with me, performing scenes from many of my favorite works. I thought we'd close with you, Tennessee. How does that sound?"

"Whatever you say, darling." The evening had just been planned as casually as it could be, but Tom was still completely unprepared. I had to protect him from failure.

I finally had something relevant to say: "We do need to locate a copy of the *Collected Essays*" squeaked out of me.

"Oh, is that where the essay can be found?" Vanessa and I were looking at each other. Her crystal blue eyes were piercing.

"Yes, I believe so," Tom answered.

I rescued him again. "*Collected* or *Complete* or perhaps *Some Essays*."

He laughed loudly, remembering he had said that to me. "It's called something like that." He looked at me and shrugged his shoulders as he laughed and reached for his wine.

Vanessa turned to Randolph. "Would you mind calling around to the bookstores to find the collection?" Randolph jumped up and walked to a phone. "We'll get it for you, Tennessee," Vanessa reassured him. I was impressed with her professionalism. She took charge and was most considerate as she did. It was exactly what this show needed.

"Good, good. Thank you, darling."

"Is that all you need?" she asked.

"Yes, I think so." Still, it all seemed uncertain to me. What if we didn't find the essay? What if he couldn't read because of his loose dentures? What if, what if …? I was worrying for everyone. Tom turned to Vanessa. "Are these people going to be good to you, Vanessa?" His need to protect her was still most important.

"Oh, I don't see why not. We're going to present an artistic event, not a political one. It's they who have made this a political issue." She spoke with confidence and self-assuredness. I knew she would make things work.

"You don't think there will be any violence, darling?" Like Big Daddy wanted to ensure Brick's happiness, Tom wanted to protect Vanessa and ensure her success to the best of his ability.

"I think we are perfectly safe. I really do," she cheerfully answered.

"Good, good." Tom was temporarily reassured.

The waiter took our orders. The conversation turned to politics when Phillip asked Vanessa her point of view on the Falkland crisis. Tom became disengaged. Politics bored him. Suddenly, he abruptly stood up.

"I have to go take a nap." He was looking at me. I knew he had already taken a nap, so I didn't know what he really needed. Perhaps he wanted to write. I took the look to mean that he wanted me in cahoots with him about needing to nap.

Vanessa asked, "Tennessee, I was hoping we might go to the theater for a rehearsal."

Tom, still looking at me, said, "Oh, darling, I must get some rest if I'm to perform tonight." He laughed but didn't move. He was waiting for Vanessa to give him permission to leave the table.

Vanessa looked at Randolph. "I suppose we could see to it that Tennessee gets to the theater later."

"Yes, Ms. Redgrave, we can have a limousine pick him up at the hotel." Randolph was always ready to execute a plan.

"Very good, Tennessee. We'll send a limousine to pick you up at 7:00. How's that?"

"Good, darling, thank you."

"Will you mind not having a rehearsal?"

I was elated that she'd asked that question and was impressed with how she let it be his decision. Someone had to take responsibility for the execution of the performance. Her tone was gracious, charming, and concerned. I wondered if she actually knew how Tom's piece would help bring the point of her show together, or if she believed he would do exactly what she needed, in spite of not knowing what he was to read.

"I think I'll be all right." He turned to me as he was leaving. "Tony, you'll see to it we have the essay?" We smiled at each other as he left.

I was stunned. Tom was gone and like an agent, I was left to figure things out for him. What if there was no book to be found? What if Vanessa didn't approve of the essay? She wouldn't be able to do anything about it. We were rapidly approaching the moment of truth. I had no choice but to believe this would all work itself out. I was ready to play my part.

The rest of us went downstairs to take Vanessa and Phillip to the theater for rehearsal. In the lobby, we encountered a group of fans who had gathered to look at the celebrities and take pictures. Randolph led the way and dealt with the crowd.

He motioned for me to come over to where he was talking with a young man.

"Tony, this gentleman says he knows Tennessee and wants to say hello!" I turned to the shabbily dressed young man and noticed he was carrying a book of Williams's plays.

"Um ... well, I don't really know Mr. Williams; that is, I know his work. I would like him to sign my book."

I was being asked to make decisions on Tom's behalf. I told the young man, "Mr. Williams will pass through this lobby at 7:00. If you are here, I'll see to it that he signs your book." It felt perfectly natural to take on the role of celebrity manager.

"Oh, thank you so much. What's your name?" He was so appreciative, so effusive.

"Um ... Tony Narducci." I felt important saying my name out loud.

"Thank you, Mr. Narducci."

I stepped into the limousine and sat next to Vanessa.

"What is your last name, Tony?"

"Narducci," I said, looking directly into her mesmerizing blue eyes. She had me under her spell.

"I thought you looked Italian. What part of Italy is that from?"

"My father is Neapolitan and my mother Sicilian."

"I love Italy and Italians." I wanted to talk more about Italy, but I knew we had a lot to do. She introduced me to the woman sitting next to her, who would play the piano at the evening's performance. Vanessa began to ask me questions about Tom, assuming I would know the answers. I was determined to help, and knew I could figure things out or make it up and still be mostly accurate. "Does Tennessee use a podium?"

I tried to imagine Tom constrained behind a podium, like a college professor. That seemed as far from who he is as it could be. It seemed to me that he would prefer to sit. "I don't think he'll need one," I said with confidence.

"Does he usually nap in the afternoons?"

I wondered why she asked that question. Perhaps she wanted to be reassured that he wasn't taking this evening lightly. "Yes, usually. He writes and naps in the afternoon."

She asked, "He doesn't look nervous or concerned about this evening. Will he be all right?" She had me there, but I couldn't let her know about my own anxiety. She needed to know that he would deliver the message without a rehearsal. She had enough to think about.

I had to believe he could do it. I had to make something up that was mostly true. "He is best when he is spontaneous. He will be brilliant tonight. We just need to find the essay." I believed what I said.

"If there is anything else we can do, please let us know. Randolph and I will make sure he has the essay." I hoped she was right.

When we arrived at the theater, the limo pulled down a long alleyway to drop the thespians off at the private back entrance. Everyone exited, except for Randolph, the driver, and me. Although none of us had read the essay or knew if it was appropriate, we were off in search of the triumphant finale that would make the point of the evening's performance. So Vanessa and Phillip would rehearse while Tom slept or typed, and Randolph and I would search for the elusive essay.

After calling every bookstore in Boston, Randolph tracked down the last copy of the *Collected Essays* to be found. It was being held at a small bookstore in Cambridge. It was rush hour in Boston. We had to navigate the knotted streets, find the Cambridge bookstore, fight off the aggressive Boston drivers, unravel the narrow horse-path streets, and get there and back in three hours. It was a daunting task. I was confident Randolph would guide us to success.

We didn't talk much. I guessed talking would distract him from his diligence. After over an hour of dodging several angry, cursing drivers, we arrived at the bookstore. As we stepped into the ancient building, the pungent scent of mold filled the air. The bookstore was cluttered with thousands of books, all of which were dusty from neglect. It felt like a scene in a Charles Dickens novel. I thought Bob Cratchit might appear from one of the tiny rooms. Instead, we found a long-haired young man sitting behind a desk, reading a book. He didn't look up when we entered. Randolph quickly approached him.

"I called about the Tennessee Williams's *Collected Essays*.

Do you have it?" I liked that Randolph took the lead. He was good at what he did.

"Oh yeah, it's in the back room." Slowly, the young man began to move. Urgency was not in his DNA. He paused to move things around as he headed for the book. I wanted to kick him.

"It was hard to find, and I think it is the last copy." Bob Cratchit talked in stream of consciousness. "I have never gotten a request for that collection. It was hiding among other works of his. At first, I thought we didn't have it because it wasn't in its correct alphabetical place, but I kept looking and found it. For some reason, it was with his plays instead of in the essay section. That happens a lot because people don't know or care where a book goes after they look at it. It's not easy to guess where someone might have left a book. I figure it had to be among other works of Williams. That's what usually happens. Sure enough, there it was, the last copy, hiding among the plays. It has probably been sitting there since it was published!"

I was overly annoyed by the clerk's rambling soliloquy. Randolph was patient and gracious. What amazing luck! We'd found the last copy, in the last bookstore, at the last minute to provide Tom the clarion to deliver the final triumphant blast at the people who fired Vanessa.

"Please hurry," I urged. The clerk ignored my request, continuing to take his time fumbling around the tiny book repository. My anxiety was growing, and I felt compelled to add, "We're expected to deliver this to Mr. Williams in an hour." I thought that the celebrity name would have some effect, but I don't think he believed me. After what seemed an eternity, we had the old, dusty, misplaced book in hand. I began to relax as I opened to the first page of the essay. I had it in my hand—but we still had the ride back to the hotel and had the evening ahead of us at the theater. There was still opportunity for something to go wrong.

The driver took the same aggressive approach back to the Ritz, zigzagging through the road-rage traffic, arriving minutes before the scheduled time to pick up Tom. I ran up to his room and found him sitting at the edge of his bed, dressed in the same faded gray suit and his tie askew but with a clean shirt. Again, I fussed over him like a doting mother. I told him we had the essay, and the limo was downstairs. We barely had enough time to get to the theater before start time. He wasn't ruffled at all.

In the lobby, we encountered a group of admirers who gathered to see the famous playwright. Among them was the scraggly young man with the book. I introduced him to Tom, and he graciously signed his book. Also, the father of a family of three asked Tom if he would mind having a photo taken with his adoring family. Tom laughed and graciously agreed, as if it were an honor. The father took a snapshot as the mother and daughter posed on either side of the revered playwright.

All beamed except me. I was anxious to get Tom to the theater and didn't understand how he could take time for all this affiliation. But that was how he was.

Tom and I got in the back of the limo, and Randolph followed in another limo. I sidled up next to Tom and put my arm around him to reassure him the evening would go well. He pushed me away and motioned toward the driver, whom he thought would disapprove of two men displaying affection. I was surprised that the man who espoused sensuality and freedom of expression would be concerned about a stranger's reaction to us, but he was a gay man of a different generation than I. We didn't talk at all about the evening or the essay. He sat staring out the window, as if we were going for a leisurely drive.

We arrived shortly before the performance was to begin. The entrance to the theater was crowded with fans and the press. The limo stopped well before the alleyway to the back entrance. That meant we had to get out in the middle of the crowd. The TV cameras lit up to greet Tennessee Williams. I panicked. What if my face was seen in the newspapers or, worse yet, on TV? I wasn't ready for the world to see me by Tom's side. How publicized was this event going to be? I had to avoid the spotlight to maintain my privacy. I opened the door on the driver's side of the limo, where most of the cameras were, and helped Tom out. Once the cameras focused on him, I stealthily exited from the opposite door. While keeping my head down, dodging all the lights and cameras, I quickly approached the entrance. Although I had escaped the press, I wasn't safely in the confines of the theater yet. At the door, a dutiful young usher asked for my ticket to enter.

"Um ... I'm with Tennessee Williams."

She smiled at me in disbelief, as Tom and the cameras steadily approached. I didn't know what to do. Luckily, Randolph appeared out of nowhere, seconds before Tom sauntered up to the door. Randolph was my knight in brown woolen armor. He rescued me. With gentle/firm confidence, he told the usher to let me in. She stepped aside, and I entered the doorway an instant before the cameras focused on Tom grabbing me to be rescued from the mayhem. I was in the theater where the cameras couldn't see me. Only my arms could be seen by the photographers.

Randolph escorted us backstage, where Vanessa was busily preparing for the performance. She and Phillip had been rehearsing all afternoon. Phillip was clutching a stack of loose papers, which were his scripts for the evening. Vanessa had everything memorized. There were costumes, lights, a piano, and a crew awaiting Vanessa's instruction. She was confident and quite capable of pulling the show together. My anxiety over Tom's nonchalance was relieved by her well-orchestrated diligence in getting things done.

Two performances of a compilation of scenes Vanessa had selected were scheduled. Within minutes of our arrival, the first performance began. Randolph handed Tom his book of essays. He tucked it in his coat pocket without opening it.

We sat backstage and watched Vanessa pour her soul into her performance. It was wonderful. Although slightly rough from little rehearsal time, the entire production was powerfully moving. Vanessa and Phillip recited poetry and did scenes from Shakespeare and Ibsen. Vanessa danced, Isadora Duncan–style. When they were done, Vanessa and Phillip exited to a roaring, appreciative crowd.

The last selection of the night would be Tennessee reading his essay. A single chair was carried out to center stage, with a single spotlight placed directly above it. Tom was standing stage right, calmly waiting to begin. He hadn't opened the book once to review the essay. Vanessa introduced him to enthusiastic applause from the audience. When he entered, they sprang to their feet, and the volume of the applause increased. Tom turned to us to smile and shrug his shoulders. We were applauding too.

As if hit by a bolt of lightning, he suddenly transformed into the eloquent titan he was. I swelled with appreciation and pride at the power of his presence. He sat down and opened the book to the essay he had chosen. The single spotlight gave him an aura of a saint. The theater was stone silent.

"This was something I wrote some years ago that I chose to express Vanessa's situation with the Boston Symphony. It is titled 'The Misunderstandings and Fears of an Artist's Revolt.'" Tom began to read. His prose came to life as he delivered each sentence with passion, highlighting passages with an ironic tone that only an artist who truly understood the intent of the prose could express. He began to read.

Why do they exist, upon what plausible basis, from what do they spring?

No rational, grown-up artist deludes the notion that his inherent, instinctive rejection of the ideologies of failed governments, or power-combines that mask themselves as governments, will in the least divert these monoliths from a fixed course toward the slag-heap remnants of once towering cities.

They are hell-bent upon it, and such is the force of their unconscious death wish that if all the artists and philosophers should unite to oppose them, by this opposition they could only enact a somewhat comical demonstration, suitable for the final two minutes of a television newscast: desperate farmers driving their pigs and goats up the stately capitol steps would be scarcely more consequential.

Everywhere tiny bands of terrorists Begin the Beguine. In the year 2013, it has been estimated that world population will be doubled. And then?

We do not wish to destroy. We are powerless to prevent.

Young, we may shout: we receive no reply but an echo. Old, we know, and know better ...

In our maturity and our age, what is there for us to do but to seek out places of quiet in which to continue our isolated cave-drawings?

Surely this is known, if anything is known by the monoliths in their (mindless or inscrutable) ongoing.

The question becomes a useless repetition.

Why the misunderstandings and why the fears?

It seems that somehow fear can exist in a monolith with a death wish: they may not want it spoken by those who still have tongues.

Perhaps we have mentioned some dangerous deceptions, in our time, and so are regarded as criminal offenders ...

What implements have we but words, images, colors, scratches upon the caves of our solitude?

In our vocations, we own no plowshares that we can beat into swords, and in our time, swords are used only for gentlemanly fencing in sports clubs or by actors in swashbuckling epics of the screen.

In a California interview, I remember once making a statement that has, in retrospect, a somewhat pontifical ring, but the essential meaning of which I'm not inclined to retract. What I said was that civilization, at least as a long-term prospect, had ceased to exist with the first nuclear blasts at Hiroshima and Nagasaki.

I have heard it said that multitudes of "American lives" were saved by these barbaric actions.

And yet I have also heard (I believe it has been officially acknowledged) that the Japanese were attempting to negotiate an all but unconditional surrender before our military command (including the genial Mr. Truman) chose to play games with our new toy, the kind of toy that belonged in, and should never have emerged from the Devil's workshop, a toy that may eventually extinguish all intelligent life yet known to exist in the expanding (or contracting?) bubble of the cosmos.

Through my studio skylight, no sign of daybreak has appeared, but work hours have grown shorter.

With the providence of luck—redundancy deserved—I'll continue after ...

After? Some hours of sleep and now again, through the skylight of my studio which, half seriously, I call the "The Madhouse," another morning's ineffable beginning, pale, very pale, but apparently unclouded. Very soon, I suspect, the rising sun will reveal once again the fathomlessness of blue.

Beginning again, it is the word "Patience" that comes into my head, and what it means to artists in revolt.

By digging in and under, they may pursue their vocation of still giving you words which they hope contain truths.

Hope? I believe they still have it.

I believe they believe more hopefully than their rulers.

Especially when they are old.

They observe while they can, the confused, the fatally wrong moves of not often evil, themselves, but forced by vested power to give support to evil.

It would seem that our childhood myths of One called God in constant combat with one called Lucifer, were an ingenuously in-carnated but nonetheless meaningful concept of the all-pervading dilemma.

It has been said by a sophist that truth is at the bottom of a bottomless well.

Many things have been said that have the ring of a clever epi-gram: fashionably cynical, yet of what use?

Oh, so many, many things have been said in a tone of graceful defeat ... And there is no misunderstanding more fearful of that tone and those sayings.

And so I presume to insist there must be somewhere truth to be pursued each day with words of an Artist, which must always remain a word most compatible with the word revolutionary, and so be more than a word.

Therefore, from youth into age I have continued and will still continue the belief and the seeking, until that time when time can no longer concern me.

As he feared, his denture bridge did loosen, at times caus-ing him to garble some words, but his essay and the delivery were awe-inspiring. The last passage made the point Tom in-tended and one that Vanessa hoped for. The artist is a trans-mitter of truth and must be free to express that truth in the endless forms it might take—like a revolutionary. World gov-ernments, any governance, should not and must not interfere with the voice of its artists. The crowd applauded wildly. Tom began to smile and cry as he slowly bowed to the generous applause. Vanessa enthusiastically approached him, hugged him lovingly, and kissed him on the cheek. She graciously thanked him and invited the others on stage to take their bows. There were three curtain calls.

In between shows, Tom and I were asked to join Vanessa backstage. We walked up two flights of stairs and entered a small, cluttered room where Vanessa was busy sorting through costumes and scripts. She wanted to change a few things before the second show and shorten it because it was late. Tom and I sat on a small sofa and watched her busily prepare. She profusely thanked him for his exclamation point at the end of the performance. He laughed with appreciation.

"Tennessee, would you like to eat after the show?" she asked.

"Yes, dear, that would be lovely."

She complimented Phillip on his work and simultaneously kept the conversation going with us as she got ready for the second performance. "How does Chinese food sound?" she interjected.

"That would be lovely," Tom answered. Vanessa had Randolph arrange for a late dinner at a nearby restaurant.

The second performance was as moving as the first. Even Tennessee's enunciation triumphed over his bridge. Again, there were loud standing ovations. Tom exited stage right for what would be his last time on a stage reading his work. An older man who had been sitting near the stairs to the stage seized the moment.

"Mr. Williams, your essay was very moving. Do you suppose your work is received as an important force for social change?"

"I don't know, darling. I just write it." Tom rolled his eyes and walked toward me. He loved to share himself with people, but he balked when he felt someone was pretentious with him, or asked him to interpret or explain his work. He grabbed my arm. "Do you suppose we could find a glass of wine?" He was wearing a Cheshire cat smile.

I laughed and told him that Vanessa was upstairs changing. She asked Randolph to keep everyone out of her dressing room except Tom and me. We joined her as she was removing her costume. She was not self-conscious or demure about removing her clothes in front of us. In fact, she undressed as confidently as she delivered her lines on stage.

Later, Tom told me that although she was a great actress, she needed to express her sensuality more. He contrasted her with Anna Magnani, whom he felt was the zenith of sensuality. He rhapsodized about the power of Magnani's ability to emote. He had a way of bringing all human expression back to a simple point: we are sensual creatures. If people didn't embrace that fundamental truth, they were missing an essential ingredient of life. Watching Vanessa undress, unruffled by our presence, was, for me, one of her greatest performances.

Perhaps I was just a starstruck fan, but in that dressing room, she exuded sensuality.

We left the theater through the back door, where the limo was waiting. Randolph made sure we were comfortably seated before we departed. Vanessa sat between Phillip and Tennessee; Randolph and I sat on the collapsible seats in front of them. With words, not bullets, we were a cozy team of renegades, united by the triumphant success of artists in revolt.

In spite of her exhausting hard work, Vanessa was energized by the receptivity of the audience and the crystallizing clarity of Tom's essay. With determination and grace, she and Tom had made her point. It was after 1:00 a.m. when the limo sped off into the night in search of a Chinese restaurant somewhere in Boston. Once on our way, Vanessa asked, "Tennessee, how did you feel about the evening?"

"It was a lovely evening, darling. I believe you let Boston know you will not be vanquished!" Tom laughed loudly.

"Thank you, Tennessee. I couldn't have done it without you. Your essay was the perfect bow on why artistic freedom is fundamental, necessary for the world to work. It would be nice to have you come to Europe with us and do the piece there."

"Oh, darling, I don't think so," Tom sweetly answered.

"Do you mind if I use your essay there?" Vanessa asked.

"Please do. I would consider it a great compliment and an honor."

Phillip made comments as Vanessa and Tom talked. Randolph guarded the group from his sentinel's post that moved 360 degrees, allowing him to keep vigilance in all directions. I reflected as the conversation continued between the two artists; it was ethereal and grounded at the same time. What had I just been part of? What impact would this have on Vanessa's career, Tom's celebrity, my life?

The limo pulled up to a fluorescent-lighted, unpretentious Chinese restaurant, filled with Asians who didn't recognize us. In one booth, however, a group of young gay men started fluttering with surprise when they realized who we were. It looked as if one of them was about to say something to us, but he was stopped by one of the others in his party. They continued to glance at us throughout dinner but didn't impose upon us. Randolph had spread his invisible cloak of protection around all of us. He waved a waitress over to our table.

We each ordered an entrée and an appetizer. There would be enough food to feed a party twice our size. Vanessa kept the conversation going by highlighting moments in the evening's performance.

"We had a packed house. It was reassuring to see Boston interested in our little production," Vanessa said to Tom.

"Darling, you were lovely. I'm certain people understood how important it is to not confuse art with politics." He laughed.

They were both very gracious. The food arrived quickly. As plates were passed, I could see Vanessa begin to nod off. Her eyes would open and close slowly as she asked to have a plate of food passed. By the time her plate was full, she was in slow motion. As she lifted her first forkful to her mouth, it froze in midflight, perched from her lovely long fingers like a tiny diving board over her plate of food. Phillip gently put his arm around her and whispered, "Are you all right?"

"Oh, yes thank you. I'm a little tired." She again lifted her fork to her mouth. This time she successfully achieved her goal. She chewed vigorously. Once again, the fork plunged into her food, once again she shifted into slow motion, and once again the tiny diving board teetered between plate and mouth. It seemed as though she had uncorked her soul, poured all her passion into expressing her point of view, and now had no energy left to eat. Phillip turned his full attention to her. He was a kind trooper. He didn't want to see her embarrass herself. He engaged her in conversation to distract her from her exhaustion. She began to eat with a quicker pace. The rest of us joined in, and Vanessa rejoined the group. We left the restaurant feeling stuffed. We were beyond tired. As soon as we entered the car, Vanessa fell asleep. Her head rested comfortably on Phillip's shoulder.

The limo moved slowly through the narrow Boston streets as it wound its way back to the Ritz. We pulled up to the entrance, and the doorman opened the door. Phillip and Randolph attended to Vanessa to ensure she made it safely in the elevator and up to her room. Tom and I followed.

With her last ounce of energy, eyes closed, she showed her gratitude one more time. "It was a pleasure working with you, Tennessee." Her voice was soft and gentle, her body resting against the back of the elevator, arms spread open for support. She looked as if she would ascend to her room without the help of the elevator.

Tom was smiling like a proud father. "The pleasure was all mine, darling. I was happy I could help." He laughed, but she was nodding off, frozen in flight like a Botticelli angel.

I turned to Phillip. "Well done," I said. "Perhaps we'll meet again, Phillip."

"Yes, perhaps we will. Thank you."

I looked for that gay glint in his eye, but he was very guarded and probably straight. Randolph was propping up Vanessa, who was now asleep in the corner of the tiny elevator cab. That was the last time I saw her. In less than twenty-four hours, I had been part of an artist's triumphant crusade for freedom of expression and the separation of art and politics. It was sublime. I walked Tom to his room.

"Sleep well, Tom." I kissed him on the cheek. Before I fell asleep that night, I reflected on how perfectly the evening had gone, in spite of my fears of disaster. Vanessa, Tom, Phillip, Randolph, and me—with her ephemeral guidance, we'd found our way.

Tom called the next morning. I sprang out of bed and prepared to meet him for breakfast. It was a beautiful spring morning. Tom was again bathed in white light in a white terry-cloth robe, reading the morning paper. I kissed him on the cheek. "Good morning," I greeted him.

He looked slightly surprised, as if to say, 'I don't know how to react when people are affectionate.' He laughed. "Yes, good morning, baby." He returned to his newspaper. I poured a cup of coffee. "There's a review of Vanessa's show in the *Boston Globe*. They're fairly complimentary of her but not so of me." He read the section that pertained to him. It mentioned the garbled quality of his voice as he read. He laughed and commented on how perceptive they were to detect his problematic dentures.

We were returning to our respective homes today. For the first time in a while, Scott would not be taking care of him. What would he do? While I ate my croissant and drank coffee, we chatted about the future. He reiterated his need to live with someone who would care for him. He was afraid of the world and felt that people would crush him if he didn't have protection. I listened but said little.

We packed for departure. At the airport, we had an hour wait before his flight to Key West. Flying made him anxious. He needed a drink to calm his nerves. We sat in the airport lounge and talked.

Tom had a great love and appreciation for the work of Chekhov. He told me he had rewritten *The Seagull* to bring out the humor more. He thought it unfortunate that most people didn't appreciate the wonderful humor in Chekhov's work.

As we talked, a young man entered the bar with his girlfriend. The girlfriend was unattractive and overweight. The young man was well-built. Tom stopped talking to nudge me and roll his eyes in the direction of the couple, who sat at a table near ours. The boyfriend was dressed in very tight jeans and an even tighter sleeveless white T-shirt. He had large, well-shaped biceps that attracted Tom's attention.

"He's much too attractive for that girl. Perhaps we should go tell him so." He laughed at his boldness.

I didn't find the young man attractive. The couple looked as if they lived in a trailer park. His face was roughed up by too many fights or nature's cruelty. He dominated and protected the young girl as if she were helpless. He was primitive. That was probably what Tom found attractive. The young man was like Stanley Kowalski in *Streetcar Named Desire*, raw and domineering, staying close to Stella, who was at the center of his world, while at the same time intent on running her life. I noticed that she was pregnant. When the young man stood up, Tom raised his eyebrows as he gazed at the boy's ass.

"He has an ass like Nureyev," he whispered. I thought the only similarity between the boy and Nureyev was the tightness of his jeans.

I once met Rudolph Nureyev at the Bistro Disco in Chicago. He was wearing a white-and-gray snakeskin jacket with matching cowboy boots. His jeans were faded blue and wrapped his body like a snake's skin. Each contour of his perfectly muscled body, especially his divine Caravaggio ass, could be seen as he walked.

"I met Nureyev at a bar in Chicago. No man's ass filled out a pair of jeans as beautifully as his!" I said.

Tom laughed and continued. "I met Rudy at a party in Paris shortly after he defected from Russia. He was beautiful but timid and frightened, like a little girl. When we were introduced, I was taken by how vulnerable he seemed. I felt I wanted to take care of him. We talked for quite a long time. He told me he was very lonely and missed his home, but he knew he could never return. My heart went out to him. My stay in Paris was short. One night was all we shared. I will never forget his ass." He laughed loudly.

The trailer park couple had departed by the end of Tom's story. I mentioned to him that his plane would be leaving shortly. Tears welled up in his eyes.

"I love you, Tony. I would like to spend more time with you. Will you take me to Europe this summer?"

"Yes, Tom, I'd like that very much." He had said the three words to me that eluded him with Frankie. I too couldn't say those words to him. I loved him, but I wasn't in love with him. I reached across the table and grabbed his hand. He was motionless. "Tom, I care about you very much, and I want to spend more time with you as well." It wasn't the three words he desperately needed, but it was the truth.

"You know, I don't respond well to affection. I was never hugged or kissed by my parents as a child." He began to cry. "I freeze when I am touched or kissed. I have my mother to thank for that. She was incapable of love. Affection would have been dishonest coming from her. I wonder if my body knows how to receive love. Although I can't provide it, I want you to know I feel loved when you touch me. Please continue in spite of my disability. I can feel my heart skip a beat when you do." He was speaking poetry to me.

"I am abundantly affectionate. I promise I will always be affectionate." I was still holding his hand.

"Well, you know, baby, in June, Harvard wants to give me an honorary doctorate degree. We could meet for that occasion and then afterwards take off for Tao Mina."

"That sounds great! I'll arrange vacation time."

"Good, baby, now take me to my airplane." I walked him to his departure concourse. "Thank you, baby." With tears in his eyes, he pulled me closer to him and kissed me. It was the first time I saw him affectionate. He always surprised, always expressed his vulnerability, always reached for, but couldn't grasp love. "I'll look forward to seeing you soon. Please continue to write me those lovely letters. I enjoy your letters very much." He smiled.

"I will, Tom. Have a safe journey." I felt sad and concerned about his welfare. I watched him walk away. He didn't look back. I wondered what he would do when he got to Key West. Would he call a friend? Would someone be at the airport to pick him up? As he disappeared from sight, I turned and walked to my gate. What should I do? What should I do? What should I do?

I wrote him a long letter when I got home. I told him how I appreciated his generosity and how much I enjoyed traveling with him. I especially loved the fun we shared, the adventures. I told him I cared about him and wanted to make him feel safe. I told him how I often felt isolated, sometimes afraid of intimacy, and how I was reluctant to fall in love—with anyone. Although I loved him for who he was, I didn't tell him that, because I knew it would confuse him. I was honest and truthful, but I didn't realize how words are defenseless in the face of raw emotion. He loved me and would stop at nothing to express it, to try to have it. I had been receiving a letter a month from him since we met, but now, I would receive a letter a week. Although I had been honest about my feelings and intentions, he held on to the hope that we would be companions.

Letter #3: You belong to poetry, Tony, not to business ...

1432 Duncan St

5/7/82

Dear Tony of my heart:

Your letter came today. It was so brilliantly written and it
touched me deeply. You belong to poetry, Tony, not to a business
concern.

I trust that we will spend a good piece of summer in England and
on the French Riviera.

I've heard that things are going well at the Goodman in Chicago.
I am finishing two plays here which I hope to place in England.
They are wild and thrilling to me as I write them.

Full of poetry-prose.

I have finished my day's work and am waiting for someone to
call me to be my guest at dinner on the beach.

I withdrew from The Miami Festival but the sons of bitches had
the audacity to say that my play was "rejected". Such things
anger me briefly but the truth will come out and I really
didn't want to play to a bunch of yahoos.

Forgive me the work-exhausted brevity of this letter.

Our Lady will bring us back together soon.

Much love,

Tom

To me, Tony, our meeting on
those stairs at "the monster"
was providential.

Vanessa is repeating her program
in Glasgow, Scotland, and asked
me to send her my essays so that a good
actor could read the piece I read in Boston.

Letter #3

1432 Duncan St.

5/7/82

Dear Tony of my heart:

Your letter came today. It was so brilliantly written and it touched me deeply. You belong to poetry, Tony, not to a business concern.

I trust that we will spend a good piece of summer in England and on the French Riviera.

I've heard that things are going well at the Goodman in Chicago. I am finishing two plays here, which I hope to place in England. They are wild and thrilling to me as I write them.

Full of poetry-prose.

I have finished my day's work and am waiting for someone to call me to be my guest at dinner on the beach.

I withdrew from the Miami Festival, but the sons of bitches had the audacity to say that my play was "rejected." Such things anger me briefly, but the truth will come out, and I really didn't want to play to a bunch of yahoos.

Forgive me the work-exhausted brevity of this letter.

Our Lady will bring us back together soon.

Much love,

Tom

P.S. To me, Tony, our meeting on those stairs at the Monster was providential.

Vanessa is repeating her program in Glasgow, Scotland, and asked me to send her my essay so that a good actor could read the piece I did in Boston.

Letter #4: I love you, Tony ...

May '82

Dear Tony:

I had hoped to find a letter from you here when I got back from Charleston - but then I thought perhaps I had asked you to write me at the Hotel Elysee in New York. I have one more southern journey to make before I go North: to a little farm in Kentucky with a house called "Falling Timbers", left to me by a painter Henry Faulkner. I plan to give it to my Vietnam-Vet friend, Robert Carroll, with whom I lived 8 years in the Seventies, sometimes pretty turbulent as he had become addicted to drugs in Nam.

Then I have to return to Key West briefly to have a permanent bridge put in my mouth where I lost three front teeth, as you may recall.

It's very late, I'm very tird, but generally better than when we last parted in Boston. I will call you soon. I do hope you can at least take me to Europe - we could meet at Harvard (Cambridge, Mass.) where I get my Dr. of Letters.

I love you, Tony, and I think there is some way that we can make it to Australia. We could do a play there - and we could play there....

Much love,

Jennifer — Jim

Inspecting a 43 acre
farm left me by an
elderly friend — It is
picturesquely (hope not
litterally) named "Falling
Timbers."

171

Letter #4

May '82

Dear Tony:

I had hoped to find a letter from you here when I got back from Charleston—but then I thought perhaps I had asked you to write me at the Hotel Elysee in New York. I have one more southern journey to make before I go north: to a little farm in Kentucky with a house called "Falling Timbers," left to me by a painter Henry Faulkner. I plan to give it to my Vietnam-vet friend, Robert Carroll, with whom I lived eight years in the seventies, sometimes pretty turbulent as he had become addicted to drugs in Nam.

Then I have to return to Key West briefly to have a permanent bridge put in my mouth, where I lost three front teeth, as you may recall.

It's very late, I'm tired, but generally better than when we last parted in Boston. I will call you soon. I do hope you can at least take me to Europe—we could meet at Harvard (Cambridge, Mass.), where I get my Dr. of Letters.

I love you, Tony, and I think there is some way that we can make it to Australia. We could do a play there—and we could play there. ...   Much love,

Tennessee – Tom

P.S. Inspecting a 43-acre farm left me by an elderly friend. It is picturesquely (hope not literally) named "Falling Timbers."

Letter #5: Lasting security as my fellow voyager ...

Campbell House Inn

1375 Harrodsburg Road Lexington, Kentucky 40504-2770

(606) 255 4281

May 26 '82

Dear Tony:

This is the letter-head of almost a life-time, it seems, of short
stays in hotels. It was to investigate a 43 acre farm left me by
an old and dear friend, a painter. I don't care to live there but
I thought it might provide security for the Viet-nam veteran who is
now sick of Chrleston, S.C. We had to drive half-way acrosst the state
to locate it. There was no h bitable house on the grounds but in about
a year it should be good acreage from tobacco and for lovely woodlands.

Soon as we got back here in Key West he looked up his old dealers and
started shooting up H. A night of hell. I hope to God he's on his way
back to Chaarleston.

I've just completed a lot of work and am exhausted but I just want to
assure you that I'd never ask you to give up a bus$ness career with
xerox unless I could offer you real and lasting security as my
fellow voyager.

It would be totally slefish of me even to suggest it.

I do hope you can take a little vacation and get me Europe, say, for a week
or two. A theatre in Syndey, Australia, wants to put on a long play of mine
but I have two other dear friends who could get me there, a lady or gentleman.
Do you like Venice? I love beach, the Lido, with the little tents alongs it
and the adjoining rooms with the sound of waves all night.

And you, dear Tony.

Things are looking up, professionally. It seems that Liz Taylor is
going to do Sweet Bird of Youth and that Liz Ashley is going to do Cat
onCable Vision.

I go to Harvard June 10th for the honoraryary Dr. of Letters. Then
I could take a Concorde to wherever you like in Europe.

Sorry to write so messily on the tired old Olivetti.

I'll call you next week whhn I go to New York.

All my love,

Tom

(Over)

lovely poster!
Thanks!

173

Letter #5

May 26, '82

Campbell House Inn
1375 Harrodsburg Road
Lexington, Kentucky 40504-2770
(606) 255-4281

Dear Tony:

This is the letterhead of almost a lifetime, it seems, of short stays in hotels. It was to investigate a 43-acre farm left me by an old and dear friend, a painter. I don't care to live there, but I thought I might provide security for a Vietnam veteran who is now sick of Charleston, S.C. We had to drive halfway across the state to locate it. There was no habitable house on the grounds but in about a year, it should be good acreage for tobacco and for lovely woodlands.

Soon as we got back here in Key West, he looked up his old dealers and started shooting up H. A night of hell. I hope to God he's on his way back to Charleston.

I've just completed a lot of work and am exhausted but I just want to assure you that I'd never ask you to give up a business career with Xerox unless I could offer you real and lasting security as my fellow voyager.

It would be totally selfish of me even to suggest it.

I do hope you can take a little vacation and get me to Europe, say, for a week or two. A theater in Sydney, Australia, wants to put on a long play of mine, but I have two other dear friends who could get me there, a lady or a gentleman. Do you like Venice? I love the beach, the Lido, with the little tents along it, and the adjoining rooms with the sound of waves all night.

And you, dear Tony.

Things are looking up, professionally. It seems that Liz Taylor is going to do *Sweet Bird of Youth*, and that Liz Ashley is going to do *Cat* for Cable Vision.

I go to Harvard June 10th for the honorary Dr. of Letters. Then we could take a Concorde to wherever you like in Europe.

Sorry to write so messily on the tired old Olivetti.

Will call you next week when I go to New York.

All my love,
Lovely poster,
Thanks
Tom

(over)

Later: This evening I had dinner with two Italian ladies from Milan, via New York. We had simple pasta—and discussed our loneliness over wine.

Now I see a play of Beckett's called *Shades*.

Alone

But he is saying alone and that brings us together,

I only wish he would indulge in a little more humor now in these later works.

Letter #6: Hoping we could work out a way for you to see me through what's left of my life ...

Dear Tony

I will get this off to you Special Delivery tomorrow.

I hope you can meet me in New York June 8th at my favorite hotel,
The Elysee, 40. E. 54th St., between Madison and Park.✗ I''ll reserve a suite there
with twin beds, hopefully my old Victorian suite. On June 9th we'll fly up
to Boston and - as guests of Harvard - stay at the beautiful old Ritz-Carlton
where we were with Vanessa the last time. Evening of the 9th there is to be
a black-tie dinner at Harvard (Cambridge,cross the river). If you don;t
have a tuxedo, please let me get you one. Maybe you should start on that
in Chicago and I'll re-imburse you when we meet.

The dotorate ceremony is on the Harvard campus the next day.

I'm longing to have a good vacation with you on the beach a6 Vanice.

Also hoping we can work out a way for you see me through what's left of my
life. With the deals on the two Lizaes set up, there should be no difficulty
unless you are realló indisolubly attached t9 that big Chicago corporation.
Must finished my second work session today and am too tired to do more than
send you much, much love.

Yours,

Tom

✗ will have my travel agent Take care
of a pre-paid Ticket for you.

176

Letter #6

Early June

Dear Tony,

I will get this off to you special delivery tomorrow. I hope you can meet me in New York, June 8, at my favorite hotel, the Elysee, 40 E. 54th St., between Madison and Park.* I'll reserve a suite there with twin beds, hopefully my old Victorian suite. On June 9th we'll fly up to Boston and—as guests of Harvard—stay at the beautiful old Ritz-Carlton where we were with Vanessa the last time. Evening of the 9th there is to be a black-tie dinner at Harvard (Cambridge, cross the river). If you don't have a tuxedo, please let me get you one. Maybe you should start on that in Chicago and I'll reimburse you when we meet.

The doctorate ceremony is on the Harvard campus the next day. I'm longing to have a good vacation with you on the beach at Venice. Also hoping we can work out a way for you see me through what's left of my life. With the deals on the two Lizzes set up, there should be no difficulty unless you are really indissolubly attached to that big Chicago corporation. Just finished my second work session today and am too tired to do more than send you much, much love.

Yours,

Tom

*will have my travel agent take care of prepaid tickets for you.

CHAPTER 6

TENNESSEE WILLIAMS AND MOTHER TERESA

CHICAGO—NEW YORK—BOSTON: JUNE 1982

After a weekend with Vanessa Redgrave and Tennessee Williams, life in Chicago was dull. Our *Revolt* got the attention Vanessa hoped for and led to a lawsuit she would later win. I wanted to live in the art world. Corporate venom was killing me.

Xerox required two weeks' advance notice to take time off. In my thank-you note to Tom, I explained the time requirement but received no reply. By June 1, I was very anxious. I called several times. No one answered the phone. I sent another note but received no reply. Finally, three days before the Harvard honorary doctorate ceremony was to commence, I received a notice from the post office indicating I had an urgent registered letter waiting for me. I thought it was my new Visa card, so I went to the post office the next day. Instead of a Visa card, it was an airplane ticket and a note from Tom, telling me to meet him at the Hotel Elysee in New York. We would spend the night there and head up to Boston the next morning. I had two days to make all the arrangements.

I devised a story about my aging Italian Uncle Tom, who had planned a trip to Italy with his sister, Rose, my aunt, but she suddenly became very ill and backed out days before their departure. The family couldn't let a trip to the homeland go to waste, so I was asked to take Uncle Tom to Europe in her place. How could I refuse? My boss was also Italian. He understood the importance of family loyalty and was very supportive. Hurdle number one was cleared.

Next, I had to get my passport updated. I went to the passport office and was told there was a one-day wait for processing. I told the agent my poignant story about Uncle Tom and his last chance to visit the homeland before he was too old to travel. Somehow, I got the new passport at 5:00 p.m. the day I requested it. I was under Tom's magic cloak. Things had a way of falling into place.

Packing for two weeks was the next hurdle. A ceremony at Harvard, dinners in New York and Boston, and relaxation in Tao Mina, Sicily, required creative costuming. In the end my suitcase was bursting at the seams.

The last hurdle required arranging for a tuxedo to be at the Ritz-Carlton when I arrived. When I explained to the hotel manager that I was meeting Tennessee Williams for an important black-tie event at Harvard University, he was exuberant about helping to expedite the request. He took my measurements and assured me it would be taken care of. I was ready to depart Chicago for the next adventure.

My flight was delayed, so I arrived New York late, jumped into a cab, and raced to the Hotel Elysee. The faded walls in the small lobby had curling, cracked paint, revealing too many layers of wallpaper. It could have been the set of *Orpheus Descending*.

Lady intended to transform her establishment from the tattered place it had become into a vibrant vineyard where she could escape the life she had come to hate. However, she was trapped in a world that threatened and frightened her and would not let her go. Freedom eluded her ... she would stay trapped in her own private hell.

Tom was dressed and ready to go when I arrived.

"We have to go now. You're so late." He turned and walked away. It was a cold, abrupt reception. There was no specified time to arrive, and the flight had been delayed. Why was he so upset? This was a side of him I had not seen. Something was wrong.

"My friend San Giorgio is having a party for me, and we have to leave immediately."

I dropped my suitcase at the front door and told him I was ready to go. He was already out the door. I felt some affection needed to be expressed, so I grabbed his shoulder and squeezed. "It's good to see you, Tom." He was distant and mute. How could he turn from the loving person expressed in his barrage of letters into an icy bitch? "Who is San Giorgio?" I asked.

"Oh, he's someone who continues to believe we have something in common."

It was the first time I heard him be so flippant. So why were we going to the party of a man he didn't like? "How do you know him?"

He was evasive. "Years, baby, years."

"Who will be there?" Perhaps some pregossip would spark a reaction from him.

He laughed and indignantly said, "I don't know. Does it matter?" He simply didn't want to talk to me. I grabbed his hand as we arrived at our destination. He wouldn't look at me. Tom rang the doorbell.

An effusive San Giorgio charmed us at the door and quickly wanted everyone at the party to know Tennessee Williams had arrived, so he announced our arrival to the small gathering. Two cheerful older women, who acted like long time friends of Tom's, were sitting on the sofa, chatting about the theater. As he entered the room, they dramatically stretched their necks in his direction, like swans looking for their reflection.

"Oh, Tennessee, it is so wonderful to see you again," one of them screeched.

The other chimed in, "We were just talking about you."

Tom didn't appear to know who they were. He was seated

in an overstuffed chair at the far end of the living room and was instantly the center of attention. I was told to sit on the sofa next to one of the chirpy women. San Giorgio handed us glasses of warm white wine.

The women kept a dialogue going about who was in town doing what play. They attempted to engage others, particularly Tom, but no one got involved. I imagined they were former stars of the New York stage who had performed in Williams plays but now were relics. Tom laughed inappropriately; San Giorgio made listener comments. I was silent and smiling. Mostly, I was ignored, which I didn't mind because it gave me freedom to scrutinize the scene. Later, I asked Tom about his relationships with the women.

"Oh, they just love to flatter me," he said.

A dinner of small salads and overly ripened fruit was served. The evening reminded me of my Aunt Angie's home. She would sit in a large winged chair, flamboyantly chatting about anything that would come into her head, telling us to help ourselves to anything we wanted. Sacks of potatoes, bags of onions, and rotting fruit were our choices. Fruit flies circled everything like dive-bombers.

After drinking several bottles of the warm white wine, other guests arrived. Phillip from the Vanessa recital was among them. How did these people know each other? A young man named John arrived, wearing a sport coat I'd seen Tom wear. I found out that John had vacated the Victorian suite where

Tom and I were staying to make room for me. I detected animosity from him.

More theater people arrived as the evening went on. It reminded me of the theater parties I attended in college—people in costumes playing "real" charades to get the attention of the celebrity guest.

Phillip, John, and I were the youngest in attendance. I sidled up to them and learned they both were struggling young actors. They were having a younger version of the conversation the two older women were having on the couch. However, instead of being critical, everything was exciting to them. Phillip brought up a Shakespeare play he'd recently seen performed off-Broadway.

"His plays are usually recited instead of performed," Phillip commented.

"That's because of the reverence some have for the 'sacred' language of Shakespeare," John retorted with disdain.

I had a bachelor's degree in Shakespearean and Victorian literature. I knew this stuff, so I jumped into the conversation. "Shakespeare was a businessman. He wanted to entertain and make money, like Ziegfeld. He knew what people wanted to see. His audience was largely the uneducated, who wanted to be distracted from their miserable lives. In a way, Shakespeare was Elizabethan TV. He offered something for everyone. He wasn't focused on making art." I was hoping to get a reaction.

"I agree," said John.

"It takes an actor who understands the intent of the play and knows the character to engage a contemporary audience," Phillip concluded.

Tom abruptly interrupted our conversation. "We have to leave." He turned and walked toward the door.

"Now?" I said softly. I wanted to continue sparring with my two young colleagues.

"Yes, we need to leave now." What was wrong? It was the first time I felt Tom wanted to control me. He ripped me away from the first interesting conversation I had since I arrived, but I shrugged my shoulders at John and Phillip and followed Tom.

A lovely woman in a mink coat offered to drive us back to our hotel. She spoke like an actress, with a deep, loud voice and perfect elocution. A handsome middle-aged man accompanied her. They could have been Nick and Nora Charles from *The Thin Man* movies. They were honored to drive Tom to his hotel. I was ignored.

In the elevator up to our room, Tom's tone changed. "Why don't you go out, baby?"

I wondered why he'd made me leave so abruptly if he now suggested that I go out. I was confused and frustrated. "I don't want to go out alone." I really didn't want to go out at all.

"Call John. He'll go out with you."

"Tom, is something wrong?"

He looked at the numbers tick away as the elevator climbed, and his response was blunt and brief. "No, nothing is wrong." His face was flushed. Days of unshaven whiskers made him look like a homeless man. He stepped ahead of me to exit the elevator. Usually, he insisted I go first.

As soon as we entered the suite, Tom went into the bedroom to take some pills. I sat on the couch, wondering what to do. I was angry that we hadn't spoken about our plans for Italy. It was selfish of him to rip me away from my young New York theater friends. I decided I would go out.

"Tom, what is San Giorgio's phone number? I want to ask John if he would like to go out." After feeling John's animosity, I didn't know why I was asking him to go out. I guess I was just trying to get out of Tom's way. There was something weighing heavily on his mind, and I didn't want to get caught in any irrational emotional behavior.

"It's in my telephone book. Look for yourself." His tone was rude and sounded annoyed. I found the number and called. Tom was in a bathrobe, urinating with the bathroom door open, while I made arrangements with John.

"I am going out with John." Inertia was driving me to go out. My tone was friendly and light. Again, I was just trying to get out of his way.

"Okay. Have a good time." He wasn't looking at me.

"Will you be all right?" I wanted him to say, *Don't go out.*

"Sure, I'll be fine."

I sounded like a young schoolboy, trying to please my teacher. In truth, I was irritated with Tom, uncomfortable about going out with John, and I needed a shower. My unpacked luggage was by the front door, where I had left it earlier when I arrived. I felt unwelcome and unwanted here with him. I'd never seen this behavior before. He was cold and manipulative. All I wanted was a shower and sleep. I walked into the bedroom where Tom was organizing several pill vials. An opened bottle of white wine was next to his bed.

"I've changed my mind. I'm not going out. I'll stay here with you. That way, we'll be fresh in the morning to leave for Boston." I thought if I could just get to sleep, perhaps this would all wash away in the morning.

He was cavalier. "Don't stay in for me. I'll be fine."

"I just don't feel like going out." I really didn't know what to say. I felt sucked into the unpredictable, being-in-the-moment life he lived. I wasn't sure how to navigate through his mood swings. I called John. "John, I've decided to stay in."

Much to my surprise, John said, "I know you slept with my boyfriend, Sebastian."

I was stunned. I didn't know they were lovers. I remembered Sebastian mentioning a boyfriend in theater. I was flabbergasted at how Tom's world was wrought with drama and full of tightly knitted intrigue, like a soap opera in which I was helplessly getting entangled.

"Are you going to deny it?" John's question felt like a threat.

I could have told him Sebastian aggressively pursued me, but I didn't want to have the conversation at all. In truth, I didn't care. I had no interest in Sebastian, other than for one night of sex. The more I said to John, the more involved I would be. I needed to extricate myself from the situation. "I'm tired, John. I need to go to bed," I awkwardly said.

"Fine. Tell Tom I'll talk to him tomorrow." He hung up.

Tom was in the bedroom. I was sitting on the couch in the living room, not knowing what to do next. I turned on the TV to distract myself from all the confusion I was experiencing since I arrived. Late-night TV in 1982 had only three channels of seedy programs. I assumed I would be sleeping on the couch, but Tom yelled from the bedroom.

"I have two double beds in here. Please make yourself at home." I entered the bedroom and fell onto the empty bed next to Tom. I thought the night was over, but Tom finally wanted to talk. "Baby?" His tone was gentle. "I want to thank you for taking me to the party and back. I really had nothing to say to those people. That's why I wanted to leave. I'm sorry if I pulled you away abruptly." He was being gracious and kind.

I felt reconnected, but I wanted to understand the petulance. "I understand, Tom." I didn't want to get into a conversation about our "relationship." I was tired and needed sleep. "Good night, Tom."

Within a few minutes, he was asleep and snoring loudly. I need tombstone silence to fall asleep and stay asleep. I got up and pulled the pillow out from under Tom's head, hoping he would stop snoring. It worked for a few minutes, but he started again. Again, I moved his pillow. This time, he got out of bed, still asleep, and started talking out loud. At first, I thought he was talking to me, but it quickly became apparent he was having a conversation with someone else.

"What do you mean, you are the greatest playwright of the twentieth century? That's not true! I'm the greatest American playwright, not you, Gene! I can't believe the audacity in ignoring me like that." He was having a conversation with Eugene O'Neill as he walked to the dresser, looking for something. Suddenly, he turned and lumbered back to his bedside. He was mumbling but still in the conversation. "Too many words, Gene, too many words in your work. I write poetry!" he said defiantly as he put a Visine bottle to his mouth and pulled the cap off with his teeth. Throwing his head back, he squeezed eyedrops into each eye. "I'm the greatest living playwright!" he garbled loudly and fell back into bed.

He was instantly snoring. I'd had enough drama for the night. I got out of bed, dragged my mattress into the living room, closed the bedroom door behind me, got into my makeshift bed, and eventually fell asleep. At 6:00 a.m., I was awakened by the loud belching sound of bulldozers from the construction site across the street. New York is full of random construction noise periodically throughout the day.

Tom came out of the bedroom and peered down at me. "What are you doing out here?"

"You were snoring. I couldn't sleep, so I set up my bed out here."

"I do not snore! I think it's very rude of you to say that!"

What's the big deal? I thought. Millions of people snore and millions of people are light sleepers. The drama continued, loudly and with indignation. He was offended.

"It's no big deal, Tom. I'm a very light sleeper." I was being gentle. He walked away, sulking like a rejected child and sat on the far end of the couch. I got up and pulled the mattress back into the bedroom. He was sitting in the same place, sulking, when I returned to the living room.

"I don't snore!" His response was assaulting, as if I had said he didn't know how to write. There was defeat in his face. What was so offensive about snoring? It seemed that any comment about him ignited his sensitivity. Was he angry because I abandoned him in the bedroom? I couldn't grasp why he was so upset. It felt so uncomfortable that I had to leave the room. He was picking a fight, but why?

"I'm going to take a shower." I bolted toward the bathroom. When I came out ten minutes later, he was still sulking in the same place on the couch.

"I can't believe you left the bedroom. Why did you do it?" He looked at me quizzically, as if I were a stranger.

"Tom, please forget it. I'm sorry. It's no big deal." I felt trapped by his inexplicable outrage at my leaving the bedroom. He got up, walked into the bathroom, and slammed the door. It was wonderfully dramatic, but I didn't know why he was acting this way. Amanda in *The Glass Menagerie* came to mind ...

"Don't you care about this family? What will become of your sister? Why do you go to the movies so often? You're like your father. What do you write about? You are always trying to escape your responsibility!" Amanda relentlessly badgered Tom. Her criticism of him was intolerable. In time, he had to leave home to avoid it.

His mother haunted him. There was no shame in snoring, yet pointing it out scratched at a wound his mother inflicted when he was very young. She must have been very critical about everything he did. I was getting sucked into the dysfunctional vortex of his life.

I got dressed and waited for him to come out. He emerged thirty minutes later, dressed in a suit, ready for travel.

"I have some business to do," he said defiantly, not making eye contact.

"Okay." I had no idea to what he was referring. I smiled and waited like a neglected, misunderstood girlfriend. For the first time, I felt I needed to escape.

"I have some checks to sign." He pulled a handful of checks

from his briefcase. "My agent sends these to me, and I sign my money away. I don't know what all I am paying for." He sat down on the couch and read each check, as if he were reading a manuscript. There were mortgage payments, donations, and support checks for his sister. A check for four thousand dollars was made out to the IRS. He read the check out loud. "Four thousand dollars to the IRS! I refuse to pay the government this amount of money! I'm an artist! Artists shouldn't have to pay taxes!" He tore up the check and stuffed the pieces into his coat pocket. He signed the remaining checks. When he was done, he returned to sulking. "Tony, I need to speak with you."

I cowered and braced for whatever was coming. "Okay, what is it?" I sat down on the sofa next to him.

"I had a stroke two weeks ago in Key West. At least, that's what my doctors say. I've been recovering. My doctors advised me not to travel. We can't go to Tao Mina. I don't see how I could in my condition." He looked out the window as he spoke.

So that was why he was acting the way he was. He wasn't able to tell me we wouldn't be going to Italy. Did he think I would reject him? I didn't entirely believe he had a stroke. I remembered Catherine's line in *Suddenly, Last Summer* ... *Aunt Vi had a slight stroke and couldn't travel that summer.*

"I understand, Tom, and I agree. We can't risk traveling at this time." The distress drained from his face. His petulance had come from fear of rejection. "Why didn't you let me know? I wouldn't have packed for two weeks." With Scott gone, there was no one to manage the details of his life. I could understand how it could slip his mind, especially if the story were true. A gnawing feeling that he was making it up to hide something crossed my mind. What did he need to hide that he had not already revealed?

"I'm sorry, baby. There's been so much going on."

I let it go. "Don't worry, Tom." At that moment, I realized I needed to guard myself from his fleeting romantic whims. He was unpredictably erratic. I began to see him in a different light. Like Blanche, he made things up to protect himself. At other times, he was deeply sincere. Unfortunately, I thought, in time I might not be able to tell the difference between what was real and what was fabricated.

We packed a few things for Boston and grabbed a taxi to the airport. Once we were on our way, Tom looked at me with tears in his eyes.

"Thank you, baby. You're good to me." He always appreciated kindness.

I wanted to get as far away from the incident as possible, so I started to ask him about people he might know to take the focus off of us. "Do you know Truman Capote?"

He laughed and with a haughty tone began to talk about Capote. "Truman is a bitch, really a bitch! He never has anything nice to say about anybody. Lovely people like Jackie O.

and her sister, Lee Radziwill, are very good to him. They have gone out of their way to support his writing, to introduce him to influential people in publishing, and show genuine concern about his welfare. He is always on their guest list for parties." He turned to look at me, as if he were about to reveal a secret. He had mischief in his face. "But Truman is good at twisting the truth. He would say they were using him because of his celebrity. As if he had anything they wanted. I think he is just a bitter old queen and a raging alcoholic. Sometimes at parties, I would see him drinking directly from a bottle of gin, guzzling it as if it was a bottled soft drink. He is always drunk."

His tone was haughty. "I don't like him very much, but he is always a great conversationalist. He goes out of his way to talk to me at parties. I listen mostly. We never engage in spending time together outside of the occasional party. He thinks being seen talking to me will attract more attention, more publicity. We were never friends. He is incapable of friendship. His narcissism renders him incapable of loving anyone but himself. But he's failed at that too. He loathes himself. After his big success with *In Cold Blood*, he didn't do much but drink and appear on talk shows. He loves to spar with Johnny Carson. He is best when exercising his wit. I think he is happy being very unhappy." He laughed at the irony.

I wanted to hear more. I changed the topic to him. "What do you think of the film versions of your work?" I felt like Dick Cavett.

"None of them are true! Characters were changed, dialogue was added or deleted, and the overall length was always shortened. They destroyed my poetry! They say it's the censorship boards. But I was thrilled to see my work transferred to film, so I went along with it. Elia Kazan was one of the worst offenders. At first, I trusted him. He attempted to collaborate with me, but in the end, we did things his way. He insisted on changing the character of Blanche. She is sensual and vulnerable. He caved in to the censorship board and portrayed her as a pathetic liar instead of a tragic romantic heroine. Her promiscuity was survival, not immorality. They wanted one-dimensional, cardboard characters. In the end, it was a Hollywood movie.

"Vivian Leigh is a good actress, but she was all wrong for the part. She was not sensual, not vulnerable, not tragic. Her performance lacked insight into the character; she made Blanche neurotic. Blanche is desperate; she's a survivor. Her actions are noble. She wanted to preserve the dignity and grace of the life she knew. Her sensibility is frail but her determination to survive, at any cost, is strong. Although her life is locked away in a sanitarium, her spirit triumphs. Kazan made Blanche a stick in a dress. I went along with it, because I had seen other great works by Kazan. Perhaps he could magically pull it together, I thought." This was a different story than what I'd read about his collaborations with Kazan. According to the press, they worked well together.

Tony Narducci

"What did you think of Brando in the role of Stanley?" I was eager to know if he agreed with the legendary flawless performance.

"At first, I was thrilled he was going to play Stanley, full of sensuality and brute force. Brando understood Stanley, but Kazan insisted on changes. Brando's Stanley went from being a noble thug to a crazed boxer. I blame Kazan for destroying my poetry!" He had tears in his eyes, as if Kazan had just told him he was casting *Streetcar* with Vivian Leigh as a helpless victim and Marlon Brando as a prize fighter. "I have been told that there is talk of Ann Margaret reviving *Streetcar* for TV. She is perfect for the part. She has all the sensuality and is vulnerable too. She doesn't look frail; she is frail. I think she'll do well."

Somehow, it seemed odd to me that *Kitten with a Whip* and Blanche DuBois could be housed in the same actress. But he was confident she was right for the part. I wanted to hear his opinion on other movies based on his work: *Night of the Iguana, Suddenly, Last Summer; Cat on a Hot Tin Roof; Sweet Bird of Youth; Orpheus Descending; The Roman Spring of Mrs. Stone; Baby Doll; Rose Tattoo.* As I thought about all of them, I was amazed at the enormous body of work that had been transferred to film. No other modern playwright or novelist could claim that many.

I asked about *Cat.* "Did you like Elizabeth Taylor and Paul Newman in *Cat on a Hot Tin Roof*?"

"Hollywood is more interested in making money than in telling the truth. If I wanted to see my work reach millions of people through the opiate of film, I had to play along. There was nothing I could do. Characters were changed, entire passages were deleted and ultimately, it had a happy ending. It was all wrong," he said with disdain. "Brick is supposed to be sexually conflicted. He doesn't entirely trust Maggie, although he defends her against his ravenous brother and sister-in-law. He knows she speaks the truth while the others lie.

"Big Daddy's part was drastically cut. Much of his wisdom and his love for Brick were left unspoken … but I do love Liz Taylor. She knew Maggie. She has all the right sensuality for my women and played vulnerability with a great deal of strength.

"You know, she and Elizabeth Ashley are interested in doing my plays. Ashley wants to revive *Cat*. I think she is perfect for the part. Liz Taylor wants to do *Sweet Bird of Youth*. She's the right age now; in fact, the role of the Princess is her life." He laughed. "Perhaps you can join me in New York when we make the arrangements."

"That would be lovely," I said enthusiastically.

He was always protean: wise like Big Daddy, fragile like Laura, gentile like Blanche, persistent like Maggie, and fickle like Alexandra. He began to chuckle as he told one more story. "You know, when we were casting for the film *The Roman Spring of Mrs. Stone*, many very attractive young men were competing for the role, among them Warren Beatty. One night while I was in my hotel room getting ready to retire, there was a knock at my door. I opened it to find Warren standing there in a white terrycloth bathrobe. I could tell he was naked underneath the robe. He asked me if he could come in to discuss the role. I knew what he was up to and told him I was tired and had to get to bed. I have made it a policy to never sleep with actors performing my work, although to this day I wonder what would have happened if I invited him in." He looked at me with his familiar wide smile. I smiled back and wondered if he was the only human being who had ever turned down Warren Beatty. I never knew if the story was true, but I understood his suspicion better. People always wanted something from him; his work was cannibalized and his truth was sanitized for public consumption.

At the height of his success, his life was emptied by loss: an absentee father, a cruel mother, a sister's escape into mental illness, his partner dead, and a world determined to exorcize his work. Yet, in spite of all that, his poetry triumphed. As I learned more about him, I better understood the source of his deep sadness.

We were finally on the plane to Boston, but we weren't seated next to each other in first class. Tom began to cry. He asked a young man if he minded changing seats with me. The young man obliged. I sat by the window while Tom and the young man shared the aisle. They chatted during the entire flight. Again, he talked this young man into giving us a ride to the hotel. It was another successful seduction. However, this chauffeur was delighted to know he was driving Tennessee Williams to the Ritz-Carlton. Tom sat in the front seat. The charming young man flattered him with appreciation of his plays. Tom acted coy, like Blanche on her first date with Mitch, pretending to be innocent but interested in seducing him, flattering him whenever possible to gain his affection. I was silent.

The manager of the Ritz remembered us from our last visit with Vanessa. We were treated as if we were family. I was told my tuxedo had arrived and was waiting for me in my room. We were expected at a cocktail party and then dinner for the honorees. We hurried to our rooms to get ready. A quick shower and a perfectly fitting tux later, I was at Tom's door to begin the next adventure.

He was ready when I arrived. A limo was waiting to take us to the home of the president of Harvard University. As the limo pulled away from the Ritz, Tom realized he'd forgotten his pills. In a panic, he yelled to the driver, "Stop, please stop!" I was startled. He grabbed my arm. He was panicking. "Would you be so kind as to go back to my room and get my pills?"

"Of course; no problem." I ran to his room and was back in a few minutes.

"Did you get them?" I pulled the booty out of my coat pocket. Tom grabbed a few and swallowed them without water, tucking the rest in his coat pocket. He never took his pills in any regimented order. I was never sure how many pills he took a day. I don't think even he knew.

Harvard had arranged a special dinner the night before the honorary doctorate ceremony for the honorees to meet and learn how the event would take place the next morning. The list of honored guests was impressive.

Harvard June 10, 1982

Recipients of Harvard University honorary degrees: 1982
Virgil Thomson, Composer
J. Donald Monan, Boston College President
Mother Teresa of Calcutta, Missionary
Dr. Maxwell Finland, Infectious Disease
Sir Peter Medawar, Zoologist
John Charles Polanyi, Chemist
Francis Hardon Burr, Harvard Corporation
Derek Bok, Harvard President
Tennessee Williams, Playwright
Wu-Fu-heng, Shandong University President
Doriot Anthony Dwyer, Flutist
Donald F. McHenry, Former UN Ambassador

When we arrived, there were photographers clamoring to take pictures of the honorees. As I did with Vanessa, I dodged the flashbulbs by exiting the opposite door from Tom. Luckily, I was in back of the cameras as they snapped shots of him stepping out of the limo. I quickly darted in the front door of the president's home, almost knocking over two very short women dressed in white-and-blue robes. At first, I wasn't sure if they were guests or if they were asking for donations. Next to them was a tall gentleman who was wearing a tuxedo with tails and white gloves. He was balancing a tray of cocktails. He asked for my name as I entered.

"Tony Narducci," I replied. "I'm with Tennessee Williams."

"Oh, of course, Mr. Narducci, welcome. We were expecting you." He directed my attention to the two diminutive women. "I would like you to meet Mother Teresa and her companion."

She was here for an honorary doctorate as well. As she extended her small, wizened hand to me, I was instantly shocked and overwhelmed with dread. Here were the hands of the saint who helped so many needy children, who blessed the people of the world, who prayed daily to God, and here I was, about to touch them. As a former altar boy, I felt unworthy of such a great honor.

With the peculiar way she extended her hand, like the paw of an obedient dog, I didn't know if I should kiss it, shake it, or bow. It didn't make sense to kiss a nun's hand, and it wasn't positioned to shake it, so I gently touched it between my thumb and middle finger, like a priest administering Holy Communion. Over my shoulder, I could see Tom approaching the door. How could Mother Teresa and Tennessee Williams share a moment? The world's only living saint with the world's most provocative living playwright: Jesus, homosexuality, miracles, cannibalism, save the children, desire—the Catholic schoolboy in me felt a mortal sin was about to be committed. I stepped aside as Tom was introduced to Mother Teresa.

"Mr. Williams, I would like you to meet Mother Teresa," the coattail-clad butler said to the honoree. When Tom heard her name, he burst out laughing, louder than I had ever heard. The sin was committed. I was overcome with guilt.

"Oh my, what a pleasure!" he yelled as if she were a football field away. The choice of the word "pleasure" seemed inappropriate, considering her piety. I could see that Tom was stunned. He bowed as if he were meeting the queen. The tiny saint had rendered the giant playwright speechless. Mother Teresa never spoke. Her companion translated her smiles and gestures into words of appreciation. The saint remained silent, stalwart, frozen at the front door with her companion at her side. She and Tom never exchanged words. All that was offered was a small hand and a big laugh.

The robe-clad nuns didn't talk to anyone the entire night. I don't think Mother Teresa spoke English, and her companion only spoke enough to be polite. I was in awe of them, steadfast at the door, warding off evil spirits, blessing the entrance as guests arrived. Tom quickly pulled me aside.

"Do you think we can ask her for a free pass to heaven?

Perhaps she has some special connection to God." He was amused by his comment and began to laugh, as if Mother Teresa had told him a joke. I was uncomfortable because people were staring at us from around the room. All of this was beginning to feel overwhelming for a street kid from Chicago. How did I get here? I felt insignificant as I looked around the room full of dignitaries and Boston's elite. I turned to Tom for reassurance as he scurried from the nuns, like the repelling of positive and negative ends of a magnet. I followed behind him as we retreated to the perimeter of the large parlor. Many of the other honorees gathered to shake the famous playwright's hand. I read the program.

I wanted to meet Virgil Thomson, who was among the select group, but we never crossed paths. As people clamored for Tom's attention, I could see distress wash over him. He turned and looked at me, wide-eyed, as if to say, *Don't leave me alone with these people.* I backed into a corner and signaled for him to join me. He was soon by my side. Unlike the premier of *House*, he didn't have to perform for this crowd because it wasn't his show. I was surprised to see him so shy.

An Asian woman and man waited to introduce themselves until the crowd around Tom subsided. The woman extended her hand and said, "Hello, Mr. Williams. I would like you to meet my husband, the president of the Shandong University in China." I was surprised she took the lead in introducing them. She was gracious and polite. Her husband bowed and extended his hand to Tom. Tom laughed. The president began to laugh as well, as if laughing at each other was customary when dignitaries meet. I extended my hand and humbly said hello.

I had never met a person living in Communist China and didn't know what to expect or say. The woman was very intent on engaging Tom in a conversation about his work. She was articulate and considerate. Both she and her husband deeply loved his plays and thought they were among the best ever written. They were sincere, not patronizing. I could tell Tom liked them. We relaxed into a friendly conversation. The president asked Tom if he would be willing to have his plays performed at his university.

Tom asked incredulously, "Would you be allowed to do that?" I think, like me, he didn't know anything about Communist China except what our Western news told us. Tom's work was provocative for a Western audience and was banned in certain places. Could it be possible that the Communist government would be more tolerant?

"Oh, I don't see why not," the president answered. "I might have to get permission, but we would be able to do it."

Tom asked, "Would the cast be Chinese?" He laughed as he asked the question.

"Oh, why not?" said the president and laughed as well.

"That would be a first!" Tom said loudly and laughed. The woman was knowledgeable about American literature, particularly his work. I was impressed with how well read she was. She wanted to know about Tom's latest play. He was obliging and told her about the premier of *House* and that he was working on several new things. After a short while, it was announced that we had to be on our way to dinner. As the honored guests made their way to the door, Tom grabbed another glass of wine. "One for the road." He laughed.

Our limo drove across campus to an administrative building, where the dinner was held. We entered a dimly lit dining hall and were quickly escorted to our assigned tables. The room was filled with faculty, patrons, benefactors, dignitaries of Harvard, and the honorees.

Tom and I were placed at separate tables at a distance from each other. He was at the front of the room. I was in the back. We couldn't see or talk to each other from where we were seated.

I was on my own and felt more intimidated by the prestigious assembly of people, without the camouflage of Tennessee Williams. What would I say or do at a table of Boston elite? Suddenly, I could hear Tom calling my name. I dashed from my seat and found him at his table, crying. He was sitting with a number of strangers. Next to him was an aggressive English professor, who was trying to "get to know him." Tom reached for me as I stepped between them.

"Tony must sit next to me!" he said loudly. I had seen him upset at the opening of *House*, but here, he was truly frightened, almost paranoiac. I think the combination of pills, alcohol, and sitting "alone" heightened his fear. He also had little regard for the conventions of an "appropriate" seating arrangement.

"Of course, Tom," I reassured him.

The professor didn't approve of my moving up from the back of the dining hall. He felt compelled to make us play by the rules. "But we have assigned seats," he reprimanded like a third-grade schoolteacher, telling us to shut up and sit down.

Tom wouldn't have any of it. I had never seen him so vehement. "No!" he emphatically asserted. "Tony must sit next to me!" He was angry and scared like a child. I felt so sorry for him. Unlike the others gathered around the famous playwright, I had seen this irrational, highly emotional behavior before. Without permission from the English professor, I stood fast between them. I was determined to protect the vulnerable poet from the rapacious, narcissistic professor. I thought of Catherine in *Suddenly, Last Summer*.

The good doctor encouraged Catherine to tell her story. "Go on, Catherine, continue."

"Cousin Sebastian ran from the devouring horde into the, hot, white sand where he grasped his heart and fell ... and, and ..."

"Go on."

"The noise was everywhere—drums, metal things, and the sound of fear."

"What happened next?"

"*They were tearing at him with sharp metal objects, tearing the flesh off his bones ... and then, and then ... they ate him!*"

I couldn't watch the voracious crowd eat Tom alive with their questions, comments, and flattery. No Harvard English professor or room of dignitaries would feed off him while I was by his side. I felt very protective. It was a behavior I hadn't seen in myself before. I think he brought it out in me.

The English professor quickly rallied and saw to it that someone at the table moved to make room for me. Once we were settled, the intrepid professor turned his attention to Tom and began to patronize. He never introduced himself to me. He thought that by engaging Tom to talk about his work, he would relax into the moment. Unfortunately, the professor didn't know that talking about himself or his work was exactly the opposite of what would get Tom to relax.

"I have loved your work for many years. I always include one of your plays in my semester's syllabus. Your interpretations of the human condition are so beautifully and tragically rendered. It's very much like reading poetry. The simplicity with which you dramatize truth and sorrow is inspiring. Tell us, Tennessee, what do you make of your work? Do you feel it has been performed and understood the way you intended?"

Tom choked out a cry for help. "Oh, I don't know. I don't like talking about my work."

"Is there anything you can share with us about where your inspiration comes from? From what I've read, it seems your family is a great source from which you draw." The persistent professor was impressed with himself and continued to ask questions, although he could see Tom didn't want to answer.

A spark hit Tom, and he ignited. "I refuse to talk about my work!" Tom's outrage was extreme, as if he had a vendetta for college professors. I think he also had a problem with authority—or at least those who posture as authority figures, like his mother. He didn't want to be badgered or interrogated. His mother had done that all his life, which caused him to leave home when he was young. He didn't want to talk about his work or where his inspiration came from. He'd also had a lot to drink. He was content to sit quietly, waiting to be fed so he could leave.

Tom's outburst made everyone at the table uncomfortable. People shifted in their chairs. They couldn't escape the onslaught of Tom's anger. He had a captive audience for this brief and painful scene. The professor was stunned into silence. People began to chat quietly.

The professor turned to talk to the woman on his left. I don't think he understood what had happened. Tom's vulnerability was scratched at until it bled. The professor never apologized for his invasion into Tom's life. He had no insight into his own behavior and seemingly no compassion. An insensitive English professor seemed ironic. I wondered what the young minds he taught actually learned.

Long before the dinner was over, Tom looked at me with

bloodshot eyes. He couldn't talk. He guzzled his wine and barely ate his food. He was ready to go home.

We drove back to the hotel in silence. Tom passed out in the limo. I was a jumble of emotions. Twenty-four hours ago, I'd been angry with him for deceiving me about why we weren't going to Sicily. Now, I was protecting him like a parent. He had the ability to draw out the entire gamut of emotion from people, both in his plays and in life.

The next morning I was up early. Tom was still asleep. A walk through the Common in early morning light illuminated everything. Different expectations about our relationship were about to collide. I saw him as a hero. He saw me as a companion. After a night of drama, I thought he would need to reenergize for the ceremony later today. I wasn't gone long. When I returned from my walk, I found him wide awake, reading the newspaper.

"How are you this morning?" I asked.

"Today should be quite an event." He was looking at the newspaper. It appeared he was talking to himself.

"What do you mean?" I wanted to connect with him on a personal level to understand how he felt about receiving the prestigious award from the prestigious university. I felt this was an enormously huge occasion for him, and I wanted to support him, but he was beyond accolades. It was just another day in his life.

"I have spent my entire life writing about what I thought

was important. Today, Harvard will bestow on me an honorary doctorate for my work." He laughed. "I didn't care much for school, never really learned much there. That ungracious gentleman last night reminded me of why I disdain it. I believe my work has revealed the truth, and I'd rather be writing about it than talking about it! Today, Harvard will tell me I did a good job. It's very ironic, you know, but perhaps I should be grateful." He looked at me quizzically.

"I'm excited. You're a hero to many people. You are to me. I'm proud of you for telling the truth."

"Thank you, baby." He laughed.

"When do we have to leave?" I asked.

"Soon, I suppose." He got up from the overstuffed chair he was nestled in and lumbered to the window to take in the light. "There is no award for a lifetime of telling the truth. I wonder sometimes if people recognize the truth, even when it's right in their face. This is an affliction I have. I write to stay alive. Yet every word I put to paper depletes my life, as if I'm running out of air. Soon, I will be unable to breathe. Fate is a wicked companion." He turned to look at me. His face was in silhouette, as if part of him was gone from his body. Only a shadow outlined where it had been.

A half an hour later, we headed for the ceremony. Tom wore his gray suit. A limo was waiting to chauffeur us to one of the expansive lawns of Harvard's campus. We pulled up backstage from where the ceremony was to be held. We had come to Olympus. All around us were the gods, waiting to ascend the stairs to Harvard's honorary doctorate degree. I walked Tom to where the other honorees were backstage, waiting to take their seats, and then I went in search of my seat. It was in the back corner, stage left and hard to find. As I sat, I could see Tom had his hands folded on his knees, like an obedient schoolboy. He looked older than anyone else on stage. His large TV-frame glasses looked like an astronaut's helmet. He stood out.

The ceremony was brief and, like a high school graduation, there were speeches and a roll call for the acceptance of diplomas. As their names were called one by one, each honoree stepped up to the podium to receive the golden fleece from the prestigious university. Each honoree had made a significant contribution to the world, in different ways, yet all meaningful in some way. I was moved. As each name was called, a brief account of the honoree's accomplishments was given. When it came time for Tom to receive his honorary doctorate, the list of accomplishments went on and on. I was so proud of him!

As the president of Harvard read the accomplishments, we were reminded of the prodigious list of great works he created. Only Shakespeare was more prolific, crafting so many recognized master works. Each title was said with sacred reverence. The audience applauded after each, as if each were being awarded individually. The combined titles read like a poem. Tom sat perfectly still.

By the time reading of the list was completed, tears were streaming down his face. I could see the white handkerchief wiping his eyes, like a flag of surrender. He was struck by what this moment meant. The world recognized him as the greatest living playwright of the twentieth century. I hoped I would hear later that he was at least a little moved by the accolade.

As Tom stood to approach the podium, I realized that no family member, no companion, no friends were here to share this achievement with him—only me, a stranger he met four months ago. Proudly, I sprang to my feet to applaud. Suddenly, the audience leaped to their feet as well. Tom bowed several times to the generous crowd. He was wiping his eyes, the handkerchief flapping in the wind and dripping with tears. While he stood facing the president of Harvard, Tom's face was illuminated with sunlight beaming in my direction, a beatific vision. It looked as if he would ascend to heaven.

After the ceremony, we headed to a luncheon for the honorees. Tom and I sifted through the crowd, dodging gaping admirers, and quickly found a table. There were no dignitaries seated next to us, only admiring and gracious fans. The sunlight brought his spirit back. He was smiling. It was a brief luncheon. We made small talk with the people seated around us, and no one tried to grill him about his work. We were merely guests like everyone else. I was thankful for that.

"I think they like me here. I am grateful they fed us." He

laughed. "I think I will take a nap when we get back to the hotel."

I had made plans with my friends Chris and Barb to meet us for cocktails in Tom's suite later in the evening. I knew they were excited to meet him. Tennessee Williams's work was the topic of many conversations we had during the time we taught at Downers Grove North High School. Tonight we would have a conversation with him.

It was dusk when they arrived. The bright golden light of morning had turned a soft twilight blue. A day of being honored put Tom in a good mood. I could see Chris and Barb were nervous when they entered Tom's suite. He sat in the overstuffed chair, flooded in blue light. He rose to greet them.

"Barb and Chris, this is Tennessee Williams." As soon as I said his name, I could see Chris blush and Barb light up like little kids opening a Christmas gift.

"It is a pleasure to meet you," all three said simultaneously. Tom graciously asked them to sit and pointed to the love seat in the window. They obliged.

"Look how lovely they look, framed in the light," he boasted. They relaxed into the ease of Tom's Southern grace. I fussed over everything: dimming the lights, ordering drinks, letting the three of them get to know each other. The scene had to be perfect: the set, lights, props, and food.

"Tony tells me you have children." I was surprised that he asked about children first.

"We have a son and a daughter," Barb said. "Our son is eight and our daughter five. Matt has just started Little League." Barb was so proud.

"I played baseball when I was a boy," Tom cheerfully interjected. "I wasn't very good at it." He laughed as Barb continued.

"It's funny to watch the boys struggle with all the athletic gear. They look like squirrels in a park, chasing nuts, when a ball is hit." Tom was interested and amused. Barb's good mothering skills endeared her to him.

"And where are your children tonight?" Tom asked.

"Oh, we have a babysitter," Chris answered.

"Mother had a babysitter for us," Tom said, "Dakin had a crush on her, and they would ignore me and Rose. I was grateful for that. I preferred the company of Rose to just about anyone else. And what do you do for a living?" he asked Chris with genuine interest.

"I'm an editor at Houghton Mifflin."

"That is quite a distinguished publisher," Tom said, as if impressed. "I work with New Directions. Have you heard of them?"

"Oh yes. I worked on an anthology that included *The Glass Menagerie*. I did extensive research on the first production in Chicago, with Laurette Taylor as Amanda. I learned quite a bit about you and the play."

"Laurette was wonderful in that role." I knew Chris would

pull interesting details out of him. "I was encouraged when I saw how easily she became Amanda. It was my first commercial success. Laurette showed me how what I wrote made sense."

"How was the ceremony today?" Barb asked.

I had to boast. "When it came time for Tom to receive his honorary doctorate, the speaker listed all of Tom's work. It was quite impressive."

Tom said, "I was humbled by Mother Teresa. There is little that compares to the great work she has done for children." I thought he was overly modest. In my mind, his body of work contributed as much to the world as her saving the children.

Tom was charming throughout the evening. After about two hours, he was tired. We drank several bottles of wine and had ordered a round of cognacs to top off the night. This was only the second time I saw him relaxed and completely engaged in conversation. Barb and Chris were kind, warm-hearted people, and so was Tom.

"I must go to bed. We have to travel to New York tomorrow. I need my rest. Tony, do you mind giving me a hand?"

I extended my hand to help him out of the chair where he'd sat comfortably all night. I walked him to the bedroom to make sure he had his medication and a glass of water and was safely tucked in bed. "I'll be back in a minute," I said to our guests. These were the little things that he loved best: being attended to, being helped to bed before the lights go out.

I wondered if his mother ever tucked him in at night or held his hand as he nodded off to sleep. I turned off the light and returned to Barb and Chris.

"How are you guys doing?" I eagerly asked. I wanted their insights about Tom and me.

"What an interesting evening," Chris said. Barb was still processing the question.

"What made it interesting?" I asked.

"He's a regular guy. He recognized the same is true with us."

"How did you read our relationship?" I knew they would be candid. Chris looked at Barb. She had great intuition and could "feel" situations. Her insights were usually right on the mark.

"He's very fond of you, maybe in love with you," Barb quickly answered.

"I think you're right. His letters have become love letters. He's drawing me into his life, and I can't resist. He's a beautiful, kind man who needs a companion who will care for him and see that his business is taken care of. He wants me to fill that role." They both knew I wanted to make films.

"So what are you going to do?" Chris asked.

I hesitated before answering. "I don't know."

"Can you continue to travel with him as needed?" Barb offered the solution I thought made the best sense for me and him.

"I have offered that. He says that's okay. But he needs and

wants more. He wants me to live with him. I can't do that. It wouldn't be honest."

"So what are you going to do?" Barb asked.

"You know, it comes down to my life versus his life. If I did what he wanted, I would be abandoning my life for his. I honestly couldn't do that. If I don't do what he wants, I am abandoning his life for mine. How do you make a decision like that?" I stood by the window, looking at the Public Garden shrouded in darkness. It was after 2:00 a.m.

"It sounds like you made the decision," Chris said.

I continued to stare out the window as I responded, "You're right, but making the decision and acting on it are very different. It would deeply hurt him if I stopped seeing him." I turned from the window to look at them. "That's what is preventing me from acting on any of this." Truth and darkness silenced us. I reached for my cognac and swallowed the last gulp.

Chris broke the silence. "We better get going; it's late."

"I don't know when I will have that conversation with him. For now, I am going to continue to support him in any way I can. If our present arrangement continues to work for him, it works for me."

They gathered their coats. I walked them to the elevator. We hugged, and they were on their way. I went to my room and passed out. The evening was branded in our minds. Chris, Barb, and I would revisit that evening for many years to come.

CHAPTER 7

THE PROPOSAL

THE RITZ: THE NEXT MORNING

We slept until 11:00 a.m. Tom called me to join him for breakfast.

"We will be leaving for New York at 3:00. What would you like to do this evening back in the city?"

"I'd like you to meet another friend of mine, John Kauppilla. He was with me at the Monster the night we met."

"Are you lovers?"

It always took me by surprise when he asked that question about one of my friends. "No, we're just friends."

"Is he attractive?"

John was pure Finnish and looked like a blond, blue-eyed Mongolian. He had a perfect nose, slightly slanted Asian-like eyes, beautiful white teeth, and a small, red tulip-shaped mouth. John was always animated. I knew Tom would enjoy having dinner with him. "Yes, he is very attractive."

"Then by all means, let's have dinner with him." He laughed. I called John from Tom's room to invite him. He was thrilled. I told him to meet us at the Hotel Elysee at six. We would go to dinner from there.

We arrived back in New York just before cocktail time. As we pulled up to the Hotel Elysee, I could see there was something on Tom's mind. I walked him to his suite. We hadn't discussed his reaction to the honor he received.

"How do you feel after receiving the Harvard honorarium?" I asked.

"Oh, I suppose it is a special award in some ways, but I am more concerned about where I go from here." He turned to look directly at me, which I took as a coy way of asking if I would be going to Australia with him.

"What do you mean?" I knew it would be about our future together.

"Tony, I would like you to take me to Australia. There is nothing for me here. The accolades don't mean much to me. I would rather start fresh in a new place with new possibilities. There are some people who are interested in supporting my new beginning in Australia. Would you like to do that with me?"

I looked at him intently, hoping he could somehow understand that this was a very difficult decision for me. It was only two months ago that we discussed our arrangement. He wanted a live-in companion. I wanted to stay in Chicago and travel with him when needed. Going to Australia would be a full-time commitment I couldn't make.

I think the Harvard accolade made him feel he was done writing plays for American audiences. Now that he won the prize for "Best Playwright of the Twentieth Century," there was no greater accolade to strive for. American critics gave him mixed reviews at best, his health was failing, his career was fading, and he was tired of the life he was living. With the determination that guided his entire life, he would reach for one last hope, and I would be his sail on the journey that would take him to the land Down Under.

"Tom, I need time to sort through my life and figure out what I want. I care about you very much, but frankly, I don't know what I would do in Australia. I still believe I have a shot at making films. I believe I could be good at it. It is the only thing in my life I have felt passionate about. I can't abandon my dream. It would be abandoning me." It wasn't what he wanted to hear.

"I know all about passion. It has been my constant companion. Most everything else is temporal. But I truly want you to be with me. I don't have much time, you know." I reached for his hand. It was lifeless. He stared out the window, as if looking for something beyond our conversation.

"When we first met, I hoped I could find my way back to film. I thought I would learn how to be an artist from you. I realize that's a path I have to find myself. How could I pursue my dream if I'm in Australia, living your dream?" That was the essential question. I knew he would see it as rejection, but it was the truth.

"I suppose they make films in Australia too. Perhaps you could find opportunities there. I know several people in the film industry. There must be some way we could both have what we want."

If a film connection was arranged before we left, I might be able to make it work, but he was very needy. Our time together revolved around his life. What would change in Australia?

"I ask you to think about it. I'll see if I can introduce you to film people in Australia. There must be a way." There were tears in his eyes.

"Okay, Tom." There was so much more to talk about before making a decision like this and it was almost 6:00 p.m.

John was on time, as usual. He looked very nervous when I answered the door. I hugged and kissed him. "Hello, darling, it's so good to see you," I said.

John waved a limp wrist of acknowledgment. "What are you going to do now that you're back in New York?" John asked.

"I don't know. I told you about the failed trip to Tao Mina. Honestly, I don't know if he is telling the truth about the stroke or if it's all drama. Now he wants me to move to Australia with him."

"What? I won't let you leave the USA. Who would I talk to

at night about my fucked-up life?" John grabbed my shoulder, as if he needed something to lean on.

"Frankly, I don't see how I could. I would be leaving my entire life behind, but I don't want to hurt him. He's so sensitive. I have to figure all this out and make a decision I can live with."

"Tomorrow is the Black Party at the Saint. We should go. You remember how fabulous it is!" John loved to party, which basically meant taking drugs, getting really drunk, and dancing all night until a dripping sweat weighed us down, and we would collapse.

"I don't want to leave him. He is going to have dinner with his sister, Rose, tomorrow night. He wants me to escort them."

John looked at me as if to say, *Whatever.*

I could hear Tom opening the bedroom door. He entered the living room with his Kabuki smile and an extended hand. John blushed red and looked to me.

"Tom, I would like you to meet my good friend, John Kauppilla."

"Pleased to meet you," said John. They were face-to-face.

Tom nestled John's hand between both of his hands. "Tony has talked a great deal about you. He was correct in saying that you are very attractive."

John laughed uncomfortably and again turned to me. I had

gotten used to Tom's blatant flirtations, but John was caught completely off guard. I had to rescue him.

"Tom, should we have a drink here or just go to dinner?"

"Oh, let's go. I could use a good walk." He was smiling at John.

"Where should we go?" I asked.

"I love the Oak Room at the Plaza. I haven't been there in quite some time. Let's go there," he gregariously decided.

"Do we need a reservation?" I asked.

"Oh no, I know several people there. We'll be fine."

I'd learned not to doubt that things would take care of themselves. We walked up Park Avenue to the Plaza Hotel.

John was his animated self and kept a constant dialogue going with Tom the entire way. Anything that came into his head came out of his mouth. John was an expert talker and a deaf listener. "The city has become so crowded. I swear it is impossible to get anywhere these days. I was packed into the subway, body to body, and believe me, some of those bodies you don't want to be close to." John loved to make flamboyant gestures with his limp wristed hands.

Tom was entertained by John's constant chatter. He began to reminisce and contribute his point of view to John's monologue. "The city has grown tremendously since I first started coming here in the '40s. I loved to wander the streets in search of adventure. In those days, the city wasn't as gentrified as it is now. Many of the neighborhoods were rundown, but everywhere was exciting."

John didn't know how to pick up the thread of the conversation, so he changed the subject. We were passing the AT&T building. "I love that Phillip Johnson building. He always uses quality materials, and the sculpture in the lobby is stunning."

I wanted to keep Tom talking, so I asked. "How have you seen the city change over the last thirty-plus years, Tom?"

"In those days, Manhattan was filled with mystery. Everywhere you went felt as if you were lost in a different city. Only the brave and the horny ventured into the bowels of Manhattan. I particularly loved to roam the streets, looking for horny sailors or a bar I hadn't been to. The city was an urban jungle, full of all kinds of hungry animals. It was exciting." As he spoke, I saw Andy Warhol approaching us. As we passed, he smiled and said, "Hello, Tennessee," but Tom either didn't notice him or ignored him. He kept walking, oblivious of the wig-wearing artist's friendly overture. John and I looked at each other in amazement at Tom's complete neglect but, we kept walking with him.

"Tom," I said, "Andy Warhol just said hello to you."

"Who?" he said with complete surprise.

"Andy Warhol."

"I don't know Andy Warhol." Tom shrugged it off as if it was nothing.

John and I shrugged it off as well and kept walking. I wondered, *Does Tennessee Williams trump Andy Warhol in celebrity?* I looked over my shoulder and could see Warhol still standing where he stopped to say hello, smiling at us, as if waiting for Tom to acknowledge him.

We arrived at the Plaza around 7:30 to a very crowded Oak Room. Tom walked up to the host and started chatting. We instantly had a table against a wall with a great view of the room. As I sat down, I saw Mike Wallace sitting at a table behind and just across the aisle from us. Wallace was known for his timely and insightful news investigations and reporting. He was one of the best in the newscasting business. He stared at us as we were seated. It looked as if he was going to stand and greet Tom, but Tom had his back to Mike. I didn't tell Tom that Mike was looking at us because I didn't know how the encounter would play out. Tom had enough interviewing for the weekend.

Mike continually glanced at us, as if calculating when it might be appropriate to say hello. Occasionally, I smiled at him, but he ignored me. He wanted to engage Tom, but they never spoke.

Tom and John kept a dialogue going throughout dinner. They were like girlfriends sharing stories about "gay" New York. Tom was in a good mood. Attractive young men always sparked his charm and flirtatiousness.

"There used to be a small bar somewhere near Broadway

and Forty-Second Street that was filled with straight sailors from all over the world. I loved going there for the challenge of converting one of them into a voracious bottom. My adrenaline would start pumping when I entered the bar, knowing it was full of possibilities. There was always someone interested in having sex. It was easier for a sailor to get a blowjob from a fag than a fuck from a bitch in heat. But I wanted the sailor boys to play the part of a bitch in heat. I loved fucking supposedly straight sailors." He told this story as if he were telling a fairy tale. His tone was sweet and nostalgic. He smiled proudly as he continued.

"A small transient hotel next door to the bar would let a room for a few bucks. Those young boys were so horny, they would gladly take the bottom position, just to have some form of human sexual contact. I loved how their tight, pink butt holes winked at me, like rosebuds waiting to be 'plucked.' Yes, I love New York." He laughed loudly, again attracting the attention of Mike Wallace, who was bursting to pop up and say hello. Tom kept talking loudly, and Mike hesitated. I wondered how Mike would feel, talking about sailors' rosebuds.

Tom continued. "In those days, gay sex was such a taboo that it made it more exciting to sneak around the darkened city in search of hot sex—so many beautiful, sweet rosebuds. The term 'safe sex' didn't exist; in fact, the less safe the better. I often imagined the police busting down the hotel door and arresting me and the beautiful young sailor I was with. The threat of danger turned up the heat. I certainly had my share of lovely fresh rosebuds."

After two bottles of wine, dinner, and cognacs, we left. John got a cab, going downtown to his tiny apartment in Chelsea. Tom and I grabbed one to the Hotel Elysee.

"Let me know about tomorrow night," John said to me as he kissed us both and was off. Tonight, there would be no argument over my sleeping on the living room couch. Tom wanted me to stay with him under any circumstances.

"John is quite charming," he said. "I bet he does well with the boys." It sounded as if he was reminiscing about his own conquests.

"He has had more than his share." We both laughed.

"Tony, I do want you to think about how to make Australia work for both of us. I understand your concern about pursuing your dream. There must be a way!"

I smiled at him. There was nothing more for me to say at this point.

The evening had been a lot of fun. I hadn't seen Tom in a consistently good mood in a long time. This was not the time to talk about Australia. I grabbed his hand. For the first time, he returned the affection. He clasped my hand between both of his and looked deeply into my eyes. I thought he was reading my soul.

"There's a way; there's a way," he chanted and clasped my hand harder, as if trying to connect with me on a spiritual level. I could feel him searching my face for an answer. I looked out the dirty taxi window and didn't say a word.

I couldn't sleep that night. This time, it wasn't his snoring. The quandary over Australia kept playing in my mind. As morning light began to creep in the window, I fell into a quasi-sleep.

I was out of bed early. Tom would sleep late, so I went in search of coffee and a croissant. It was a warm, bright June morning. The streets were full of people starting their day. This was the time I liked New York best. In the early light of day, the tattered shell of the great city showed its new world strength. Solid stone buildings, carved by unknown craftsmen, were built to stand the test of time. The intricate limestone carvings were the signatures of the artisans who made them.

The narrow crosshatched streets were bordered with an occasional ginkgo tree, reaching its oddly shaped geometric arms up to the sky, like the abstract art that was born in this city. Somewhere I read that ginkgo trees are one of the earth's oldest living life-forms, with a completely impervious immune system. How appropriate that the city that was built to last would grow the tree that would never die.

As I meandered aimlessly through this monument to American ingenuity, I thought about Tom. The genius who unmasked so many truths of life to a sensually starved world deserved to live the last part of his life with love and happiness. I wanted to give something back to the man who gave so much. But what about my needs? I feared I would lose myself in caring for him. What would my life mean when I was seventy if I didn't attempt to reach for what I wanted? I was young; he old. Perhaps I could carve out a piece of my life for him. My mind swelled with indecision. After a coffee, a croissant, and soul-searching walk, I headed back to the hotel. I arrived midday to find Tom watching TV news.

"Would you like to go to lunch?" I asked.

He didn't respond to my question. He was intently watching the TV. "The world is getting worse and worse. I don't like Ronald Reagan as president. He's not genuine. It's as if someone winds him up, and he delivers a prerecorded message. He is the worst kind of person to be a world leader. He's an actor—and a bad one at that. Actors are best when they are performing. His presidency is a performance. Bette Davis once told me he was a simpleton. He has no depth. What did you say, baby?"

"I asked if you would like to go to lunch."

"Oh yes, that would be lovely. I want to take you to my favorite Italian restaurant in New York, Nello. It's the best Italian food outside of Italy. I'll get ready."

"Do we need a reservation?" I should have known better than to ask.

"No, I know the people there." As we got ready, I continued to weigh my options. Perhaps I could give him a year. I would need a salary that I could save to fund my film projects.

Asking for money might hurt him. Maybe that would put me in the category of con man. The more I ruminated, the more confused I became.

We arrived at Nello to an effusive Italian welcome. It seemed that everyone working in the restaurant knew him and genuinely cared about him. It was as if he was truly part of their family. The host knew what kind of wine he drank and asked if he wanted the usual pasta and graciously included me in the conversation. I felt at home. In a quick scan of the menu, spaghetti carbonara jumped off the page. Few Italian restaurants serve that dish. After taking Tom's order, our host turned to me.

"Spaghetti carbonara, please, and a glass of white wine, same wine Tom is having."

The host happily replied, "Yes, of course. Would you like anything to start?"

Tom remembered a dish he liked. "Oh, why don't you put together one of those lovely antipasto trays you do so well."

"Of course, Mr. Williams. Antipasto, my pleasure." He bowed twice and scurried off to place our order.

"I love Italians!" Tom said effusively. "They are so warm and full of life." He was smiling at me. I began to feel uncomfortable. I knew what was coming. "Tony, I love being with you. What can we do to make this work?"

I felt caged. "Time, Tom. I need to figure out my life in Chicago." I knew I was being evasive.

"Time is what I don't have much of. That is why I need to know what you think."

I couldn't look him in the eye. Instead, I looked down at the table. I was at a loss for words. After an awkward silence, I began to piece together the beginning of a negotiation for our lives. "I am torn between what you want and deserve, and what I need to find out about my life. How can we do that together?" I was hoping he would see the dilemma as I did and come to some shared point of view.

"I imagine two smart fellows like us can figure it out."

We had this conversation many times and had made little progress. We were dancing around the real issue. He was content to believe we were headed in the direction of Australia, and I let it pass. Scratching at me for a decision would push us toward a collision. The truth was, I was unable or unwilling to say I didn't think Australia would work for me because I didn't want the adventure to end. I was getting frustrated with my hesitation in confronting this issue head on.

The antipasto arrived and diverted our attention from the conversation. Cured meats, roasted porcini mushrooms, soft cheeses, and fresh vegetables served with crispy, crusted Italian bread and a rich extra-virgin olive oil were divine.

My carbonara was a perfect medley of creamy sauce, pancetta, peas, and al dente pasta. Our host insisted we have tiramisu and sambuca for dessert. The tiramisu was like eating sweet, light clouds. The sharp, sweet licorice taste of the liqueur melted with the tiramisu to create ambrosia in my mouth.

Tom wanted to go to a bar near Nello for an afternoon glass of wine before his nap. We crossed Park Avenue and entered a small corner bar. It was empty so there was nothing to distract us from the overwhelming indecision that was becoming an obstacle to enjoying our time together. Tom was very uncomfortable. I believe he was afraid of the coming rejection, though I had no intention of rejecting him. I wanted to make it work for both of us but was at a loss to know how. We each ordered a white wine and sat in silence for a while.

"I made a reservation at Windows on the World for 6:30," said Tom. "Rose will arrive in a limo at 6:00 to the hotel. It's always difficult to take her out in public. She is shy and needs a lot of maintenance. I think she may have a friend with her." He was looking at me and smiling. The storm about our future had passed for now.

After our drinks, I walked him back to the hotel and helped him into bed. I sat in the living room, reflecting on whether we were any closer to a decision. I felt constrained and frustrated. When I felt this way as a young boy, I would run away. Usually, that meant staying with a friend or relative until the feeling passed. My life as a child was full of constraints. There were six of us living in a tiny two-bedroom apartment, with no place for privacy and no money. My father used fear to discipline us. I never knew when I was going to get yelled at or hit for some unknown reason. Escaping the constraints of my family life meant freedom. I did it frequently. That same feeling was taking hold of me because Tom was pressing me for a decision. I felt I needed to run away.

As I continued to ruminate, I remembered what John said about the Black Party at the Saint tonight. I felt the need to take flight well up in me. Impulsively, I decided to escape this quandary. Without thinking of the consequences, I quickly packed all my things and headed downtown to Chelsea.

John's apartment was located across from the Church of Saint Francis Xavier on Sixteenth and Sixth. From his seventh floor apartment window, the giant downward-facing head of Christ on the cross loomed in front of us. His torso and outstretched arms perfectly framed and filling the tiny window gave me the feeling God was watching us. What had been sacrificed between Tom and me by my running away? His hopes, my dreams, and some sort of relationship were all colliding in my mind. I was overcome with guilt at my impulsive escape.

John loved miniature things: eyeglasses, furniture, buildings, buttons, and anything else he could find in miniature. The Thorne Miniature Rooms at the Art Institute in Chicago were his favorite things on earth. His apartment was like one of those miniature rooms. It was no more than 450 square feet, with a closet-sized kitchen, a closet-sized bathroom, and a lofted closet-sized bedroom. A library-type staircase climbed up to the attic cube, which was filled with John's life in boxes. There was no air conditioning, and it was hot as hell. He didn't use the lofted bedroom because it became a lofted storage area instead.

I could never sleep when I stayed there. The noise, the heat, and no air conditioning made it intolerable. There was only the small Christ-facing window that created the illusion of space. We each slept on a twin-sized futon at the perimeter of the tiny living room. The walls had no insulation or soundproofing.

His neighbor was into heavy metal music that he would play loudly after midnight and continue until dawn. John's attempts at quieting him repeatedly failed. It was purgatory at best. Years later, just before John died, he said the heavy metal neighbor was found dead in his apartment with the music blasting.

I arrived to a warm welcome and the excited anticipation of a night of debauchery. I think John was secretly proud of the fact that he'd "stolen" me away from Tom. John was not only the most loyal person I have ever known, but he was also one of the most possessive. He protected and kept me close to him whenever we were together. Although we were only friends, he felt closer to me than any other human being in his life. I loved him for that. At about 5:00, the guilt that I'd abandoned Tom made me call him to tell him what I had done.

"Hello," a somber voice said.

"Tom, it's Tony," I said reluctantly.

His voice perked up quizzically. "Baby, where are you?"

"I am at my friend John's—you remember, from dinner last night."

"Oh yes. When are you coming back? Rose will be here soon." I was swollen with guilt and regret. I couldn't say the words, "I'm not joining you." Instead, I said, "I am going to go to the Black Party with John."

He was instantly enraged. "*What?* You're a con man, just like all the rest!"

"Tom, please understand. I needed to get away to think."

He had already hung up the phone. I was paralyzed with anxiety. What had I done? I was at a pay phone near John's apartment because I wanted privacy when I had this conversation. I walked around Chelsea for an hour, trying to understand my own behavior. I came to no resolution, so I returned to John's.

"I think I hurt Tom."

John looked at me and said nothing. At that moment, I realized I had never spoken to anyone about how I felt about my experience with Tom, or how I felt about him. All I shared were the stories. I certainly never talked about my intent or where I thought this relationship was going. I was living it moment by moment. I didn't know what to do.

"What are you going to wear?" John asked. I deserved the flippant response. I had done nothing to let my friends think that this was anything more than an adventure. I hadn't thought of it as anything more than that, until now.

I sat on the floor and buried my head in my hands. "I really think I hurt him."

Now John could see that I was truly upset. He tried to comfort me. "You're just taking a break. Can't he understand that? It will be fine; don't worry." He meant well and that was the right thing to say, but I felt awful. Tom had told me how difficult the evening would be, and I abandoned him. I was silent most of the rest of the night.

I eventually rationalized that I had done it because I was concerned the press would be there, taking pictures. Trapped in a booth at Windows meant no easy escape from the flashing cameras. I was supposed to be in Italy with my uncle Tom. How would I explain this to my boss? I feared being fired, but that rationalization didn't last long; I had let him down.

John and I both wore all black to the Black Party: shoes, socks, belts, and tight, tight, tight jeans and T-shirts. We looked like ninjas, dressed like everyone else—an army of ninjas. I hated looking like everyone else, but the Black Party was inspired debauchery, and the black outfit gave us the rite of passage into the ritual.

We entered the lobby of the once grand vaudeville palace to the loud pulsating beat of phenomenal house music. The building was shaking from the blasting bass. John saw to it that we snorted plenty of cocaine before we arrived, and there was plenty more to keep us flying all night. We were strapped in for the ride.

As we approached the downstairs center stage, I could see a beautiful, naked young man performing a provocative interpretive dance, with a large anaconda snake held by the head between his legs. It was flailing in all directions, as if it were the boy's tail. Five nearly naked well-built men, dressed in black leather head masks and tight black leather jock straps, surrounded the boy. One of the men took the snake from the boy, while another put him into a sling, allowing him to be swung from masked man to masked man. The boy performed fellatio on each man as the others held him in place. It was richly decadent.

More cocaine and we headed for the amazing, out-of-this-world dance floor. It was shaped like a flying saucer, suspended in the large open space of the theater, hovering as if it were in a docking station. It was designed to transport us to another galaxy far, far away. We climbed the stairs to enter the dance space.

Inside the flying saucer, a white dance floor floated in a white mist. The ceiling of the dance floor was a white perforated scrim that allowed the space to breathe. Light filled the space like air. All the whiteness was like a dream in another dimension. Dressed all in black, the revelers looked like insects trapped in a giant white bubble, wriggling in dance to escape this distorted dimension. It was fantastic! Inspired! Transcendent!

The ubiquitous loud music made it impossible to talk and be heard. The space was designed for insular all-night dancing. The music, the drugs, and the crowd of hot, sweating men ignited our libidos and intensified the craving for sex. We danced ourselves into a delirious frenzy, like ritualistic warriors in a kiva, preparing for battle. There was nothing like this on the planet.

After hours of nonstop dancing, we needed a break. We tore ourselves away from the ritual and headed for the balcony. John spotted an attractive young man staring at us.

"Let's take him up to the balcony and see what happens," John lasciviously suggested.

The balcony of the Saint was designed for rampant, orgiastic, unsafe sex. The seats had been removed, leaving wide expanses of carpeted, ascending platforms, suitable for spreading out and having any sexual activity imaginable. We took John's young man to the balcony. I felt awkward, fondling a man with John. We were brothers. It seemed perverse. John got into it, and I retreated from the threesome and began to look at the orgy taking place all around me. Everywhere, there were naked men having sex. No one used condoms.

The decadence of this scene blew away the confines of "normal" sex with one partner at a time. Men were obsessed with voracious, all-consuming sex, with as many partners as could be fit into the space of a night. Public group sex was at its zenith in those days. Gay men didn't know how this was fanning the all-consuming flame of HIV that would devour thousands of gay men in the years to come.

While John was finishing his anonymous encounter, I went downstairs to watch a different young man in the sling perform the snake-and-masked-men ritual. None of this was worth leaving Tom and Rose on their own for dinner. Although I was always intrigued by these events, I got bored quickly. I couldn't have public sex, and I could only dance until I got tired of the loud, mind-numbing music. This scene was pervasive throughout New York in those days. This would be the last Black Party I would attend.

We left at 4:00 a.m. and walked home. John was still high as a kite and rambled on about everything: the hot guy in the balcony, the absence of people late at night on the streets of New York, how the Saint was the most high-tech, advanced dance bar in the world, the amazing architecture, and on and on and on. I loved him dearly, but I just wanted him to shut up.

We arrived back at his place to the neighbor's blasting heavy metal music. I was infuriated and still buzzing from all the coke. It seemed there was nowhere in New York where I could get a good night's sleep. Exhausted, frustrated, and feeling guilty, I collapsed onto the tiny futon. I don't know that I ever fell asleep. I was in a numb daze until I got out of bed at 7:00 a.m.

I left New York midafternoon. The adventure with Tom was becoming a drama that I had to escape. I idolized him but didn't want to be his permanent partner. The intensity and depth of Tom's complex emotional life, his age, and his neediness were not something I could handle. But I had let this involvement happen. I had a responsibility to make amends. When I returned to Chicago, I wrote a letter of apology. I wanted to reconcile some type of friendship.

CHAPTER 8

MEA CULPA

CHICAGO: JULY 1982

I called my boss to let him know that my trip with Uncle Tom had been canceled. I explained that in a fit of anxiety, he decided he couldn't go on the trip without his sister Rose. My boss bought it because he had bigger things on his mind. Xerox had decided to rethink their "go-to-market-strategy," which was code for cost-cutting and downsizing. He was in the middle of deciding who would stay and who would go. I really had no idea where I would land in this restrategizing effort, and in truth, I didn't care.

BlueCross BlueShield Association in downtown Chicago was my biggest client. Shortly after I returned to work, I told my client, Larry, that things were changing at Xerox and that I might be leaving. He told me he had a consultant position available and offered me the job. Starting a new position in business was not the direction I hoped my life would go, but I couldn't get off the money-making machine.

My new job promised more money and the freedom to design my new role as I saw fit. For the first time in my career, I was in control of the work I did. I would truly be a consultant; researching, designing, and developing learning experiences, as well as providing executive coaching, management development, and building salespeople's consulting skills. However, the biggest bonus was that I would be making training films. Not exactly the kind of film I hoped to make, but it would be a start. Within a couple of years, I would be promoted to director of the department, where I would have more opportunity to be creative, make more money, and would be free to experiment with new approaches to consulting, which included making more films.

It took several days to compose a letter to Tom that explained my point of view about my hasty departure from Hotel Elysee that day. I reiterated that I was willing to be companion and friend and happy to accompany him on business trips. I protested his accusation that I was a con man. I reminded him I was and always had been an admiring fan who truly appreciated spending time with him. I reminded him that I hadn't asked for anything, especially money. I told him I thought his reaction to my backing out of dinner with Rose was like an eager soldier confidently stepping on a land mine—he had not thought before acting. I apologized for not following through on my commitment to help him manage dinner with Rose. I regretted not meeting the only person he called family. Within the confines of the truth, there was no more I could say. However, what bothered me the most about my behavior was that I contributed to his overwhelming feeling of loss. Like so many before me, I had abandoned him. The seeds of compassion Tom had planted in me were now blossoming into the full realization of the pain of loss. I sent the letter and waited for a reply.

Taking another job in the business world instead of pursuing a career in filmmaking told me that my certainty about returning to filmmaking had eroded. Could I find meaning and fulfillment in the business world? If I made more and more money, would I have more and more freedom, more happiness? My soul didn't believe a business career was a meaningful way to live, but for the first time in my life, I was able to spend money. Fancy dinners, designer clothes, extravagant trips, posh hotels, and lots of things to buy were all very seductive. I loved being able to freely spend money. Never in growing up in Little Italy did we have extra money to spend frivolously. My parents were barely able to pay the bills.

The way I looked at it, earning money provided opportunity for more choices, and choices allowed for a better life. In rationalizing my decision to continue working in the business world, I wondered if I was becoming one of the people I held in contempt. My life was headed in a direction I never expected and didn't know that I wanted. It also further illuminated the truth about my relationship with Tom. I knew from the beginning that I couldn't be the constant companion he so desperately wanted. I needed independence to make my own money, buy my own things, and make my own decisions.

Our "breakup" made me reflect on what was really going on in my mind between Tom and me. I realized that I saw our relationship as a series of isolated, existential adventures, not connected to my mainstream life and really not connected to each other. Each adventure was a special moment that I enjoyed immensely, but it was like watching a movie. I was observing my time with Tom, but I wasn't in it. The truth was, I wasn't in love with him, and I couldn't sacrifice my life for his. However, I had to see him one more time to let him know how I felt … and then I got a letter with an opening line right out of the poetry in his work.

Letter #7: At best, reality is a matter of varied interpretations ...

Dear Tony

At best, reality is a matter of varied interpretations. Forgive me for
reminding you that you would not share a twin bed two nights in a row
but removed living-room pillows to floor for sleeping, complaining that I
snored.

I prefer adjoining rooms but when I have had vriends in a twin bed bewide me,
none has complained of my snoring.

Then you informed me first you were spending that last night out. I accepted this
with regret but composure. Then you called to sa/ you would not even lend your
assistance to me for the always difficult dinner with Rose and her 88 year old
companion - well, I have sensibilities and they can be wounded.

I don't regard you as a con man but $ remarkably less considerate than your
letters had led me to expect.

You would abandon me in Venice after one week !   Thanks nbut no thanks....

I am not bitter. I simply think you should face the other side of the situation.

Letter #7

Chicago: July 1982

Dear Tony,

At best, reality is a matter of varied interpretations. Forgive me for reminding you that you would not share a twin bed two nights in a row but removed living-room pillows to the floor for sleeping, complaining that I snored.

I prefer adjoining rooms, but when I have had friends in a twin bed beside me, none has complained of my snoring.

Then you informed me first, you were spending that last night out. I accepted this with regret but composure. Then you called to say you would not even lend your assistance to me for the always difficult dinner with Rose and her eighty-eight-year-old companion—well, I have sensibilities, and they can be wounded.

I don't regard you as a con man but remarkably less considerate than your letters had led me to expect.

You would abandon me in Venice after one week! Thanks, but no thanks …

I am not bitter. I simply think you should face the other side of the situation.

Tom

At best, reality is a matter of varied interpretations. In a few words, he described our relationship. We were experiencing our time together from different perspectives. I was having a series of existential adventures. He was writing me into the story of his life. It was hard to interpret the poetic letter's tone. Did he want me to respond, or was this how it would end, with no end? I ruminated. Should I respond to the letter or end the drama without a final scene? I needed to see Tom in person one more time.

My life was moving faster than it ever had. Freedom of choice became a ride I couldn't get off. I didn't know where I was going or what I was looking for. When I was driven by my desire to be a filmmaker, I knew what I wanted. Now, all I knew was that I was making money, and I liked it.

My new office was only six blocks from where I lived. I could walk back and forth to work, like a kid walking to school. It seemed that my life was beginning to have purpose—not the purpose I'd hoped for, but nevertheless purpose. However, I still had to find meaning in what I was doing.

That summer was hot and sticky. The window air conditioners Danny and I bought were noisy and did little to cool our apartment. At night, they rattled so loudly it was impossible to sleep. Our downstairs neighbors were three guys—two brothers and a friend. They were loud and stayed up all night talking and goofing around. Our choices for sleeping were either to let the rattling bedroom window air conditioners drown out the neighbors' noise or to listen to the young men exercising their testosterone. At times, I would yell downstairs through the window well, *"Shut up!"* They always ignored me.

Eventually, late at night, the noise would cease, and I would fall into a zombie state of quasi-sleep. This was when the monkey birds would come out, making that horrifying screech that frightened me as a child. I never saw them, but their monkey-like screeching would instantly awaken me. I would be transported back to the first time I saw *The Wizard of Oz* at the age of six. The scenes with the flying monkeys dressed like hotel bellboys terrified me. I imagined being lifted out of my shoes by long, curled talons and carried off to the witch's castle. Once awakened, the six-year-old could never fall back to sleep.

It was the first summer of the "gay plague." A virulent strain of pneumonia was raging through the gay community like a wildfire. Some doctors were saying that gay men might have a gene that brought on this condition. Those doctors were practicing homophobic bigots who expressed their hatred in grandiose doom-based condemnation of the gay lifestyle. Other hate-filled people were pleased to see God doing his work by killing off the gay sinners. Not yet knowing what caused this health crisis, gay men went about having endless promiscuous sex. We had no idea we were fueling the AIDS fire.

I dated many different men that summer and never practiced safe sex. Like so many gay men, I was ignorant of the reality that was unfolding around us. As baby boomers, we were living in the afterglow of penicillin invincibility. Little did we know that random oblivion was our constant companion. Most of us would survive, but thousands would get sick and die a horrible death.

One of the longer relationships I had that summer was with Garrison, a ballet dancer from the Chicago Ballet Theater. He was tall and elegantly built, with curly blond hair and blue eyes. I called him *Gabriel.* He looked like an archangel with Da Vinci blond curls. His long arms and big hands made him look like he could fly.

Garrison also heralded the coming of doom for me. After many weeks of unsafe sex, he told me his doctor had diagnosed him with something called ARC—Gabriel the ARC angel. One day, he casually told me that his immune system was suppressed by this condition. He said it wasn't contagious. At first, I didn't know what to make of this announcement, so I ignored it. A week later, he told me his doctor wanted to see me to test if I had contracted anything. I was furious with Garrison and told him to fly away.

After a series of tests, the doctor found nothing wrong with me but asked me to come back once a month for testing. The National Institutes of Health (NIH) was launching a five-year study to monitor the health of one thousand gay men across the country. The intent was to track the progress of the disease, in hope of developing better treatment or prevention. At that moment, my life went into a deep freeze.

I stopped being promiscuous and waited anxiously for what I thought would be my death sentence. I recruited five friends to join the NIH study with me. We received free check-ups twice a year. Of the six original friends I asked to join me, only Darryl and I would survive. We watched so many beautiful young men rot away and die horrific deaths. Our world caught fire and it blazed for fifteen years. I thought of Tom's recurring fear, *"I don't have much time. I'm going to die. I don't want to die alone."* I now thought I too was going to die soon.

In time, Garrison and I would learn that we were HIV-negative. I would see him at parties from time to time, but I never trusted him again. It wasn't as if he maliciously withheld the truth from me. None of us knew about the raging pandemic in the early days. I was angry about all of it, and he was my scapegoat.

Eventually, I wrote Tom a letter, asking him about the intent of his last letter. Were we reconciled, or was he too hurt to see me? I dropped the letter in the mail and received one from him two days later. It was too soon for him to have gotten my letter and to write one in return. Serendipity had again played a hand.

Letter #8: The Last Letter – I've learned to exorcise jealousy from my nature. It is time ...

4/27/82

Dear Tony:

I was disappointed to find no letter from you here when I returned a coupla days ago from Sicily and Rome. I had assumed that – from our varying viewpoints, scarcely irreconcilable – we had dismissed whatever tension developed in New York.

The chances are that I will be back in Chicago this season as I have completed a play on which I worked three years, MASKS OUTRAGEOUS, and Greg Mosher says there may be an open slot for it at the Goodman. He would be very obtuse, which isn't like him, not to make one. He's not yet read the play.

Peg Murrry of HOUSE NOT MEANT TO STAND is planning to direct that one in the New York area.

Are you totally pre-occupied with a new lover? I put nearly all my amatory impulses into my work. An Irish lady, large of body and heart, is in residence here, keeping the house well-organized, having been associated with The World Bank in Washington, D.D.

Let me hear from you, Tony.

Love,

Tennessee

Your letter had arrived in this afternoon's mail! Of course I'm delighted at your release from Xerox Come down here! – we will discuss a future together.

I'm learned to exorcise jealousy from my nature. It is time.

253

The Last Letter: #8

8/27/82

Dear Tony:

I was disappointed to find no letter from you here when I returned a couple days ago from Sicily and Rome. I had assumed that—from our varying viewpoints, scarcely irreconcilable—we had dismissed whatever tension developed in New York.

The chances are that I will be back in Chicago this season, as I have completed a play on which I worked three years, *Masks Outrageous*, and Greg Mosher says there may be an open slot for it at the Goodman. He would be very obtuse, which isn't like him, not to make one. He's not yet read the play.

Peg Murray of *House Not Meant to Stand* is planning to direct that one in the New York area.

Are you totally preoccupied with a new lover? I put nearly all my amatory impulses into my work. An Irish lady, large of body and hair, is in residence here, keeping the house well-organized, having been associated with the World Bank in Washington, DC.

Let me hear from you, Tony.

Love,
Tennessee

P.S. Your letter had arrived in the afternoon's mail. Of

course, I'm delighted at your release from Xerox. Come down here! We will discuss a future together.

I've learned to exorcise jealousy from my nature. It is Time.

CHAPTER 9

AN HONEST CONVERSATION?

CHICAGO—KEY WEST: EARLY SEPTEMBER 1982

"Hello?"

I was surprised he answered the phone. "Hello, Tom. It's Tony." My tone was cheerful and friendly. After all the drama we had been through, I hoped we could be friends—or at least friendly. My letter was clear on how I felt, but we wrote each other simultaneously, so I didn't think he understood my point of view. A line in his letter troubled me: *we will discuss a future together.* What type of future did he mean? I felt we might be back where we started.

"Tony, baby! How are you?" He was thrilled to hear from me.

I had to be cautious. Although we spoke the same language, we interpreted the words differently. "I'm fine. How have you been?"

"Oh, I'm good. I have been very busy with travel and writing, you know. It's how I live my life." He laughed his always-familiar laugh.

"I want to come down to Key West and spend some time with you, talk about things, and have some fun." It was the clearest I could be. It was simply the truth.

"Yes, yes, of course. I was hoping you would come down. When do you suppose you would be here?"

"I thought I would come down for a long Labor Day weekend. How does that work for you?"

"Good, good, that will be fine. Let me know your flight arrangements. I will pick you up at the airport. I have learned to not be possessive." His tone was jovial, but the words confused me. He still wanted something more from me.

"I will call you soon to let you know my flight arrangements. Look forward to seeing you in Key West," I said with genuine enthusiasm.

"And I you," he said and quickly hung up the phone.

I was going to Key West with the best intentions but without the gift he wanted most—my heart. I hoped we could come to common ground, but to him I was the reincarnation of Frankie. I hadn't seen him since June, and we'd last talked on the phone in mid-August. I hoped we could reconcile our differences, but I had my doubts.

I called him when I arrived. Outside the terminal a perfect blue-and-white hot day greeted me in Key West. I could hear the waves splashing against the shore. The rhythmic hula from the wind in the palm trees welcomed me back. At a distance, I could see Tom's car entering the airport. A large blonde woman was sitting next to him. Tom was wearing a wide smile and a bright yellow shirt. The woman was dressed in all black in the late afternoon, scorching-hot tropical sun.

Tom had a big smile on his face and a gracious greeting. "It is so good to have you back in Key West. We have prepared the upstairs room for you. I will give you a key, as I am sure I will be going to bed well before you," Tom said. "Tony, you remember Helen. I believe you met in New York." Helen had been in the lobby of Hotel Elysee when I arrived on our way to the Harvard honorarium in Boston. I had no idea how much a part of his life she was. What was her role? I had never spoken to her, and Tom never talked about her. She must be a good friend of his, I thought. She was easy to remember because of her size and the platinum-fried hair that was too long for a woman her age.

"We did. How are you, Helen?"

"Fine," she said coldly, avoiding eye contact and saying nothing else. I instantly felt she hated me.

I turned my attention to Tom. "Thank you, Tom. I appreciate your hospitality."

"Of course, baby, of course. I thought we would drop your things off at my place and then head out for cocktails and dinner."

Oh good; the tone of our conversation was upbeat, but

why the cold shoulder from Helen? "That sounds great!" I said. "The short plane ride seemed to take forever in the tiny, mosquito-in-the-wind aircraft I flew on. Drinks always ease anxiety."

"I know. I have made easing pain with alcohol a way of life!" He laughed. Helen remained silent and didn't say a word all the way to his house. Her rudeness wouldn't interfere with my having a good time, or so I thought.

When we arrived, Helen awkwardly exited the car. Her large, round body dressed all in black was aggressively unattractive. Tom graciously waited for me to gather my things. He escorted me into his home, like a gentleman pampering a lady. By the time we entered, Helen had disappeared. Tom directed me into the kitchen, where his maid was cleaning up. She was old and looked as if she had been doing this work for centuries. She lumbered around the house, looking for something to pay attention to.

"Leoncia, I'd like you to meet Tony."

"Why, it's a pleasure to meet you, Tony." Kindly and gently, she extended her ancient, frail hand to me, smiling as if she were greeting a family member. She barely grasped my hand, but her warm spirit touched me deeply.

"It's a pleasure to meet you too." Her warm personality was in sharp contrast to the other woman I would be sharing this moment with.

Tom was looking at me as if he was proudly presenting a

newborn baby. "Doesn't he look like Frankie?" That meant she had been his maid for a long time. Being compared to Frankie didn't have the charm it once did. After our conversation at the Ritz bar in Boston about their "open" relationship and Frankie's never telling Tom he loved him, I didn't think Frankie was an honorable man.

"Why, yes, he does; he looks like Frankie." Laughing and running a towel across the countertop, happy to be included and eager to please, she made me feel at home.

"Would you like something to eat, Mr. Williams?" Like a permanent fixture in the kitchen, she continued her chores.

"Oh no, thank you, we are going out."

She hobbled away from the counter and opened the refrigerator. "Why, there is plenty of food here. Why don't I make you something?" She was in her element. It was easy to see she had devoted her life to taking care of people—it was her joy.

"That is very kind of you, Leoncia, but I am sure Tony is eager to get outside into this beautiful weather after being cooped up in that nasty airplane." He was right. Being outside in the hot, salt-infused air was just what I needed.

"It was nice to meet you, Leoncia. Perhaps I will see you again while I am here."

Smiling and sincere, she fixed on me as I exited the kitchen. "It was so nice to meet you too." She flashed a smile and returned to wiping the counter. "I am sure you will."

Tom was already walking toward his bedroom. "I need to

take a couple of pills." I followed him into the bedroom, where he sorted through pill bottles. I noticed on his dresser a silver-framed black-and-white photo of Helen, taken when she was much younger. I was surprised to see it there because it wasn't there on my last visit.

She was beautiful then. What happened? I wondered if Tom had known her for many years. Perhaps she recently gave him a picture of herself when she was younger, or maybe Tom had the picture for many years and recently put it out because she was staying with him. Either way it was bizarre. A photo on a bedroom dresser usually denotes that this person is someone very special, like a family member or a significant other. What was the relationship between Tom and Helen about? She had to be someone he trusted. I hoped she was good to him. I never found out anything about their relationship. I guessed she was there to fill the role Scott vacated—and I didn't want.

"Oh, Tony, let me show you your room. Helen is staying in the guest room adjacent to my room—you know the one you stayed in last time." Why was she staying in an adjoining room? Did she care for him in the middle of the night? Was there some form of intimacy between them? Perhaps she had trouble climbing the stairs to the attic bedroom. Again, I never found out. "Upstairs, you'll have the attic all to yourself. That way you can come and go as you please." He was gracious about ensuring I felt no constraints.

"Thank you, Tom. I feel very welcome." I was behind him,

ascending the narrow staircase to the attic. The room was small and dark but cozy, in a cottage sort of way. It was also very hot. I knew I would have trouble sleeping.

"This is lovely. Would you have a fan to cool off the room?"

"Yes, of course, baby. I know it can get quite warm up here. I'll show you where it is."

I dropped my bag and followed him downstairs to a closet where there was a fan. I grabbed it and quickly carried it upstairs to cool off the room. Without unpacking, I returned to the living room to await our next move. I could hear Helen stirring in her room. She must have been waiting to hear Tom's voice before she exited, not wanting to risk having to be alone with me. Tom appeared from his bedroom, dressed in a fresh shirt and smiling ear to ear.

"I thought we would go to a place on the water to have a drink. I like to watch the light fade from the Gulf. It turns darker shades of blue as the sun sets." He was standing in the middle of the room, scanning it as if looking for something. "Where is Helen?" As soon as he finished his sentence, she opened her door and bolted into the room. A lightweight black shawl had been added to her black ensemble. It looked as if she were going to a late-afternoon funeral.

"Oh, Tom, are you ready to go?" Ignoring me, she waddled to the door.

"Yes, let's go. Helen, do you mind driving? I want to be free to talk with Tony."

"No, I don't mind." I could see she was irritated. Not only did she have to tolerate me, but she also was required to make it easy for Tom to pay more attention to me.

"Thank you, dear. Shall we go?"

Helen was already out the door. Tom graciously motioned for me to go next. Once we were settled in the car and on our way, it struck me that everything I did with Tom would most likely include Helen. I had to pretend she wasn't there.

"So, Tom, what has kept you busy this summer?"

Before he could answer, Helen blurted out, "Where are we going?" She completely disregarded the conversation I was trying to have with Tom. I thought she was being deliberately rude to me.

"Oh, let's go to the Sands for a cocktail and see where the evening takes us from there. That's a perfect spot to watch the fading light."

Helen had trumped me in having a conversation with Tom. Expedience was more important than reunion. She was in control, and I would have to wait until Tom turned his attention back to me. Completely ignoring me, she continued to take control. "Oh, I love that place. I hope we can get a table by the water. There's always a good crowd there, and the food is so good."

"Yes, dear, I love that place too. Tony, do you know the Sands?"

Coincidently, it was where John and I had dinner the night I met Tom. Should I seize the conversation by diverting attention to that first night or just answer the question? I stuck with expedience. "Yes, I have been there several times." I only answered what was asked. I knew Tom would pick up the cue.

"And do you like it?"

"Yes, I like it very much." My answers were crisp and to the point. Tom would figure out the drama of the evening without my having to act like a jealous girlfriend.

Helen was pulling into the parking lot of the restaurant as I spoke my last word in answer to Tom's question.

"Here we are," she blurted out and quickly opened the car door. I watched her struggle to release herself from the bondage of the steering wheel. Tom slowly emerged from the front seat. I was already waiting to help him out and down the path to the restaurant. Helen charged ahead to be the first to arrive, in order to ask for a table by the water for Tennessee Williams. It was a ploy to get a strategic seat at the table, one where she would be the center of attention. We were behind her as the host looked from her to us to verify that TW was in fact here.

As soon as he recognized Tom, he said, "Right this way, please, Mr. Williams." We were quickly escorted to the best table in the house, with a perfect view of the Gulf, the sand,

and the elusive, fading light. Tom and I sat on one side of the table and Helen on the other. She immediately began to devour the menu without taking a bite. I helped Tom into his seat; then I sat.

"I think I'll have a salad," she said without anyone paying attention.

"Let's have champagne!" Tom announced, laughing and smiling.

Finally, some alcohol, I thought. Perhaps that will put a different spin on the evening. "That sounds perfect," I said. I wanted Tom to take back the evening from Helen.

She reinserted herself. "Oh, Tom, let's get the champagne we had at the bar the other night. I love that brand. What was it?"

"Oh, I don't remember. Get what you like." He turned to me and rolled his eyes as Helen tore open the wine list to find what she wanted. "Tony, what would you like to do while you're here?" Tom asked.

At last, I thought I would have a conversation with just Tom. "I would like to relax, go out to the bars, get drunk, and stay out late, and of course, I would like to spend a lot of time with you."

He laughed loudly. "Of course, baby, of course. We'll have breakfast, lunch, and dinner every day. Would you like to do something else?"

I wanted to say, *Yes, I would like to do something without Helen*, but instead, I said, "It all sounds great."

The waiter came up to the table, and Helen ordered the champagne she wanted. I retreated into the flow of wherever the conversation would take me.

Tom was in a good mood and began to talk about how Key West had changed over the past few years. Helen was in constant agreement with whatever he said, as if she had lived here since the 1940s as well. She aggressively kept herself connected to him throughout dinner. I made mostly "listener" comments to show I was paying attention, which I wasn't.

After dinner, Tom looked tired. "I would like to go home," he said. "Helen, perhaps you could take Tony out on the town." He was looking at me. "He did say he wanted to go to the bars and get drunk." He laughed. Going out with Helen was exactly the opposite of what I wanted to do, but I said nothing, neither accepting nor rejecting the idea.

Helen picked up on the awkwardness of the situation and took charge, mostly to appease Tom. "I would love to take Tony out on the town." She was a good actress. There was no way she wanted to take me out, besides I didn't need anyone to escort me. Key West was like a second home to me. Most importantly, I didn't want to be seen with Helen. I wondered what kind of reputation she had here. If she treated me so poorly, she had to have rubbed a few people the wrong way. I looked down as she spoke to avoid eye contact with either of them. I knew they would read reluctance in my face.

"Thank you, darling. Tony, is that all right with you?"

I had to respond. I picked up on his direction to Helen. "I would love to go to a bar and get drunk." At least that was the truth. I didn't make any reference to how I felt going out with her.

"Good, good. You two have some fun." We walked to the car. Tom was moving slowly. I could tell he was tired. I really wanted to go back to the Monster with him, alone. Since that was where it all had begun for us, I thought that would be a perfect setting for our heart-to-heart talk. I thought it best to have that conversation at the beginning of our time together, so we could relax into our redesigned relationship, instead of after any drama happened. I closed his car door, and off we went to take him home.

I walked him to his front door while Helen waited in the car, vigorously applying lipstick. Did she think she would be kissing someone tonight?

"Good night, Tom. I look forward to breakfast," I said.

"As do I. Know that I will sleep late but nevertheless look forward to seeing you sometime in the morning … or after-noon." He laughed.

I had been in Key West for less than six hours and so far, this was not the visit I hoped for. Instead of finding common ground with Tom, I was playing hypocrite to a woman I would never hang out with in my world.

Key West was not like the real world. Thousands of people came here every year because it was a place where they could dream and be encouraged, no matter how ridiculous the dream or how much of a loser they might be. It's what made Key West special. With Tom safely home, we were off to a night in hell.

I didn't know how I would have a conversation with Helen. I wanted to be sarcastic, flippant, and find all the ways I could to make fun of her, which would be easy for me to do. However, I realized I probably couldn't make her feel any worse than she already did. I couldn't be cruel. I decided I would let her take the lead tonight; that way, I could see more of who she was. There had to be a point in the evening where I could slip away.

As soon as Helen drove away from the house and out of Tom's hearing range, she started talking loudly about where she wanted to go and how much fun it was. She might as well have been talking to herself. She wasn't interested in what I might want to do.

"There is this place on the conk side of town that's getting a good crowd." The conk side of town referred to the west end of the island, where the indigenous people lived. Her tone was friendly, as if she were talking to a girlfriend. I was surprised how easily she flipped into friendly mode after being so rude.

"I've never been." My tone was neutral. I had no reason to dislike this woman. Perhaps she thought I was trying to take her place in Tom's life. She was trying to make this a competition for Tom's attention. She entirely misread me. It was then I realized she was threatened by me. If I took her place at Tom's side, where would she be? I had no intention of doing that. There was so much we didn't know about each other. I wanted to extend an olive branch, but then the plot thickened.

She took us to a place where the locals hung out, west of Duval Street. This was the first gay bar on the native side of Key West I had been to. We pulled up to an ancient outdoor building painted screaming pink, exploding with ear-shattering disco music. The place was too ostentatious for me. I decided to have a drink and figure out a way to leave her. Helen insisted on sitting at a table where there was plenty of room to gather people around her. When the waiter came to take our order, Helen said, "Oh, I have no money. Do you mind buying me a drink or two?" She looked directly at me, with her eyes bulging like a late-night rodent.

I thought, how dare she come to a bar with no money? Does she think someone will buy her drinks, as if she's a beautiful twentysomething? I was pissed off. This was the type of behavior some cute, young gay men use to get someone to buy them drinks. Older men were easy prey for an adorable, needy boy acting interested in them. It could work for young boys but never for her. Her request was completely inappropriate. I knew then that Tom paid for everything, and she expected the same from me. Perhaps she was a female con man.

Was Tom supporting her? Of course he was. I was invading her territory. She thought I was trying to take her meal ticket away, and she would defend her turf to the death. This behavior was stereotypical in the gay community. I avoided people like her in Chicago. Why should I endure it here?

"Don't you want a drink?" she asked.

Hell no, not with you! I thought. But, instead, I bought each of us a white wine as the first step toward walking away from her. When the drinks arrived, I put a twenty-dollar bill on the table and stood up to walk away.

"I know what you are up to with Tom," she said bluntly.

I felt angry and wanted to say something cruel. Instead, I thought of Tom's constant grace in the face of brutal intent. I nonchalantly said, "Oh?"

"Every man he has spent time with, has wanted something from him. What do you want?" It was as if she read the script from Act I that first night at Tom's. Those were his words, which she didn't know he had spoken to me. Either she was speaking the truth and had lived through all the con men with him, or she too had heard him deliver that line and knew it would get a reaction from me. I wasn't going to play into her hands.

"I want his friendship, nothing more," I said sincerely.

She looked at me as if I was lying. She wore a smirk that said she had heard it all before. Nothing will convince me that you're not a con man. "Friendship means a lot of things," she said sarcastically. "What do you mean?" I was impressed with her persistence. Perhaps she was looking for the truth because of a sincere interest in protecting Tom, or perhaps she was looking for a way to protect her claim on him. Either way, I had no interest in having this conversation with her. I stopped talking. There are times when words just don't communicate.

I was gracious. I guzzled my wine and smiled at her. It's what Tom would have done. "Good night, Helen, and thank you for taking me out. I know we'll see a lot of each other this week." I dropped another twenty-dollar bill on the table. She looked at it and then at me. As I walked away, she had the last word.

"Thanks, I'll see you later." She, too, played it as Tom would have.

I quickly put all thoughts of Helen aside and walked to the other side of the island. It was dark. The conks were hanging out on corners. They would quiet down as I approached. I was an interloper. They stared at me until I was out of sight.

I was soon on Duval Street, heading to the Monster. At last, I was on my own. I wanted to relax, get drunk, have sex, and some fun. It was like having a prescription filled. The

Monster was the pharmacy. The booze and boys were the drugs.

The Human League song *Don't You Want Me Baby* was blasting as I arrived. The pulsating music felt like electricity racing through my body. I ordered a glass of white wine and began to scan the crowd. Within a few minutes I noticed, a dark, well-built Cuban guy smiling at me. He didn't look gay. He oozed a macho sensuality. He smiled and winked at me, signaling he thought I looked delicious too.

I walked up to him and started talking. "I just arrived from Chicago. I'm Tony."

"Carlos." We shook hands.

The night was hot. I could taste salt and sex in the air. We were soon dancing. Shirts came off. Glistening in the moonlight, we rubbed our sweaty bodies against each other, releasing the spirit and igniting the libido. I lifted myself onto the bar, where I began to strip, liberating my body from the confines of the day. I was down to my tight white briefs in minutes. Carlos was watching hungrily.

I pumped and gyrated, until I attracted a small audience. I thought of Tom saying, "We are sensual creatures," as I proudly displayed my tan sweat-drenched body. Surprisingly, I was not kicked out. Perhaps people thought I was hired entertainment. In those days, it was "anything goes" in a disco dance bar. After three songs, I jumped down and put on my clothes.

Carlos was besotted with desire. He scrutinized my body as I dressed. It thrilled me to feel like a whore.

"My friend has an apartment at the other end of Duval," he said. "Do you want to go there?"

I looked up at him and smiled yes. "Of course I would."

He smiled back as we walked to the exit. He had an old, faded blue Jeep. Within minutes, we pulled up to a rundown, beige-paneled two-flat apartment building. A single naked lightbulb at the top of the stairs cast dark shadows on our faces. The building looked like a duplex trailer home. Carlos led the way up the single flight of unpainted stairs. The light made Carlos's dark features and sunken eyes look like a demon. The setting and tone were perfect.

The apartment was stark white and full of beds. There were at least four in the living room alone. I thought this might be a depot for illegal immigrants until they found a place to go.

He played the aggressor. As we began to reach an orgasmic crescendo, the front door opened and another sexy Cuban man entered the room. He instantly started a conversation with Carlos as we had sex, as if we were having lunch. The interloper quickly undressed and joined us. I left after releasing all my pent up anger and took a taxi back to Tom's. I never saw Carlos or his friend again.

When I got to Tom's, I inserted the key into the front door and gently turned the knob. The inside door chain was latched, preventing me from entering. This was Helen's work.

I climbed the fence into the side yard. Jiggling the glass patio door easily opened it. I was in the house in ten seconds without waking anybody.

The next morning, Helen was shocked to see me. By the time she got out of bed, I already had told Tom that I was locked out. Together we waited to confront her.

"Why did you lock me out of the house last night?" I bluntly asked.

"I didn't lock you out of the house," she protested, ignoring me as she looked at Tom.

"Darling, I don't see why you would lock Tony out of the house," Tom casually said.

Helen looked apologetic and hastily went to Tom's side of the table. "Maybe I unconsciously locked it when I went to sleep." I could see *liar* all over her face, but I wasn't going to argue with her. The woman offended me, but I was stuck with her as long as I was in Tom's home. She knew I was on to her, and she would do her best to stay at the center of Tom's life.

I went out every night, and every night I arrived home late to find the door locked. Every morning, Helen would rise to be surprised to see me in the house. She never learned how I got in, and I never mentioned it to Tom again. Defeating her was good enough. She could lock me out of the house, but she couldn't lock me out of his life.

I got in about 4:00 a.m. each night and slept until noon. Tom wanted to write in the afternoons. I went out every afternoon to enjoy the sun and the scores of naked men at the various guesthouses across the island.

My friend Albert had bought a large old Cuban mansion on Fleming Street. He moved from Chicago to Key West in the late 1970s, when the first wave of entrepreneurial gay men came to wake up this sleepy island. He turned the mansion into a guesthouse called the *Jasmine Gypsy*. Scores of gay guesthouses opened up in Key West in the late '70s and early '80s. Most of them were sex palaces, accommodating hundreds of young men looking for fun, relaxation, and bountiful sex. The *Gypsy* was rundown but in a great location, with its original old-world charm and splendor intact. There was six thousand square feet of space, with several sleeping rooms and a large swimming pool. It was a perfect refuge.

On other visits, Albert would let me stay there as long as I slept with him. We didn't have sex; he just wanted to cuddle. Albert was always gracious. He sold the Gypsy in 1982 for a lot of money and bought a smaller, tucked-away house that was much more manageable and didn't have any guest responsibilities.

I went to visit him a couple of times while Tom wrote. Albert was an industrious, multitalented man who, over the years, had gotten into renovating old homes, painting, catering, and making stained-glass windows that he sold at a local art store. I was always impressed with his many talents.

I stayed in contact with him because he was a kind, generous man. Unfortunately, people took advantage of him. When he owned the *Gypsy*, several young men stayed there rent-free. They did little to earn their keep. It never seemed to bother him. He was the Auntie Mame of Key West, taking in young men and supporting them until they were able to take care of themselves. I didn't realize this would be one of the last times I'd see him. He would die of AIDS a few years later.

Each night, Tom, Helen, and I would go out early to dinner to watch the sun set, drink wine, and listen to Helen patronize Tom until we were all completely bored, including Helen. Tom and I never got a chance to be alone. In fact, I never talked with him without Helen present for the rest of the trip. When I asked Tom if we could go out to dinner without her, he would say, "I don't see why not." But each night, she would be there. Tom would let it slip by. I think she feared that if I were alone with him, I would turn him against her. She was always with him. I think he liked the devotion. It seemed to me it was a codependent relationship. She provided companionship to the fearful, aged artist who didn't want to be alone, die alone. In return, he provided her a free ride. We were three misfits trapped in an existential moment with little in common and little to share. I felt held hostage by the tenacious control of the desperate faded beauty. After dinner, I would drive Tom and Helen home and take Tom's Jeep out to the bars. I always danced half-naked and would meet someone to have hot, meaningless sex with.

On my last night in Key West, Tom planned a special dinner outside of old town Key West, at a dive bar with a small restaurant above it, much like the set of *Orpheus Descending*. The ransacked shack looked like it had been there since the pirates came to bury treasure. I hoped it would be just the two of us, but it wasn't meant to be. It was my last night, and I was determined to have the needed conversation with Tom, but I didn't want her to witness what was personal between the two of us. We would have no time together to talk. I would leave Key West with no thread to pull our relationship forward. The trip would be like visiting my aging aunt Angie. Instead of fruit flies dive-bombing over rotting potatoes and onions, Helen hovered over my time with Tom, leaving our relationship to rot due to the absence of meaningful conversation to nourish it.

The restaurant had few tables. It accommodated no more than twelve people. When we entered, six people were already in the tiny pirate's nest. Tom knew the owner and chatted with him until Helen said she was starving. We turned our attention to food.

Dinner was as usual. Helen and Tom talked about former glories, gossiped about people I didn't know, and seldom engaged me in the conversation. At times, they seemed like competing women, trying to outdo each other with stories of their travels and conquests. They liked hearing themselves talk, even if the other wasn't listening. I was attentive but disengaged. After dessert, Tom turned his attention to me.

"Tony, the time has come to talk about our trip to Australia." He was looking directly at me.

I was stunned. I flashed back to his last letter, *We will discuss a future together.* I thought we had put Australia behind us, but he wanted me to join him under any circumstances. I was about to let him down again.

Having this conversation in front of Helen told me she was relatively unimportant to him in the long run. Talking about our future in front of her meant he had little regard for her place in his future, if I would be there. I didn't want to have this conversation with her watching us, but I had no choice. I even had more empathy for her now. It was clear that she was just a placeholder until Tom found a companion.

"Since I arrived in Key West, I've wanted to talk to you about our relationship, but we've never had time to ourselves," I humbly replied, searching for a way out of having this conversation with Helen present.

He was determined to know where I stood. "Any time is the right time to talk about your life," Tom wisely added.

I couldn't deflect answering the question. I hadn't heard much about Australia other than he wanted to start a new life there. So I asked, "What are your plans for Australia?" I leaned in to the table and peered into his eyes for an answer that would help guide me through this conversation. I don't think he wanted to talk about it. He just wanted me to say yes to ease his fear of loneliness. I could feel a familiar sadness welling up in him.

"Oh, I don't know. There are a couple of theaters there that are interested in my work. I would like to launch some of my new plays there. The critics here are too mean. In Australia, I can start fresh."

I thought he was kidding himself, but I couldn't say that. It would crush him. I didn't see how he would have greater success in a different part of the world. For years I listened to friends tell me how much they hated living in Chicago because it held them back from doing what they wanted. I would say to them, "It's not the place that gives you a life; it is what you do. You can't escape yourself."

I wanted to say to him, "New York, Los Angeles, Chicago, Sydney can't make you happy. Happiness grows inside of you and not from the roots of a different place," but he had to know that better than I did. I could feel our connection slipping away. I struggled to help him help me see how this move would benefit both of us. "What would we have to do to prepare for this move?"

"Buy a couple of airline tickets, book a hotel, and go." He laughed as if it were that easy. It sounded to me like the adventuresome spirit of a nineteen-year-old sailor going on furlough. He was too old to cast his fate to the wind, and I was too young to have a fate or a wind to carry it.

Helen sat there, her eyes bulging like a bullfrog's. I wanted to throw her into the middle of a large pond and watch her sink. She said nothing, but I could see victory on her face. I imagined Helen's frog tongue instantly extending across the table to grab me like a fly and swallow me in triumph. Tom was smiling, intently looking at me for my answer. I couldn't hedge anymore.

"Tom, I have grown very fond of you. I love you, but not in the way that you want to be loved. I can't go to Australia with you, Tom. I would be sacrificing my life for yours. It would be dishonest of me to go if my heart wasn't in it."

He looked directly at me as I spoke. The smile never left his face. As he reached for his wine, he began to cough, as if he were choking on something—the truth, perhaps. He was drowning in loss. When he was finished coughing, the smile returned to his face.

"Well, then, I guess it is time to move on." His response was nonchalant, without question or discussion. After almost a year together, it seemed he would have put up more of a fight. Gentility prevented him from fighting for what he wanted, or he had no fight left in him. As we rose to leave, I could see he was crying. This time they were gentle tears. There were no sobs, no gushing waterfalls, no grief—just sadness. I wondered what he meant by "it is time to move on." What he really wanted from me was to be loved, the same as he'd wanted from his mother, from Frankie. I had let him down, just like the others.

We drove back in silence. Even Helen kept her mouth shut. When we were parked at Tom's house, I said, "I have an early flight in the morning. Should I call a cab?"

"That would be best, baby. I don't do morning very well." I thought his choice of words poetic. Did he mean he didn't get up early in the morning, or was it that he fell apart when he was mourning?

I walked him to his bedroom. He asked me to get him a glass of water. I scurried to the kitchen and quickly brought him the water. He was sorting through pill bottles when I returned. I handed him the water.

"Oh, put it on the dresser, baby."

I did as he asked. "Can I help you find something?"

"Oh no, it's right here." He was distant. Words eluded me. "I'm tired, baby. I need to sleep."

"Will I see you before I leave in the morning?" I asked.

"Peek your head in the door to say good-bye," he said without looking at me.

"Tom, you have always been good to me. I want you to know that I appreciate your kindness, and I care about you."

He turned from his pill search to smile at me. "Thank you, baby. Good night."

"Good night, Tom." I wanted to hug him, to reassure him I would still be in his life, if he wanted. We could get as drunk as sailors and enjoy each other's company as we had before. But instead, we were dissolving into the truth of the differences between us. He was at the end of an illustrious life; I at the beginning of an uncharted one.

There were no con men here, no sycophants. Just two people struggling to find happiness in their own way. I left his room and closed the door behind me. As I climbed the stairs, I wondered who had been *the kind stranger* these past eight months—me or him. What I didn't know was that this would be the last time I would see him.

The attic bedroom was hot, and I wasn't tired. I ruminated about the evening, the last few months with Tom, and how uncertain I was about my life. The more I ruminated, the less I was able to sleep; the less I was able to sleep, the more I ruminated. The last thought I had before fading out was that I had made the right decision. Although my life was moving away from filmmaking, I had come to terms with my new reality. I would use all my wits to make a career in the business world work. If I went to Australia with him, I would be bored and anxious in no time. Most important, I knew I couldn't mislead this great man. I couldn't take responsibility for his life if I wasn't responsible for mine first. I hoped things would work out for me and for him.

I got out of bed early. The house was still. I showered, packed, and went downstairs to wait for my cab. Tom's and Helen's doors were closed. I started to turn the knob to his bedroom door but stopped when I heard him snoring. I decided not to disturb him. Before I left, I took a slow scan of the house. Everything was a little dustier and frozen in time. The only thing that moved was the lazy bulldog. I was escorted out of the house the way I was escorted in, with the old dog leading the way. I pulled the key to his house out of my right hip pocket and gently placed it on the countertop in the kitchen. It never had opened the door to let me in. I left a brief note:

> *Tom, thank you for the time ... I hope you find*
> *what you're looking for in Australia. Love, Tony.*

I quietly left the house, stepped into a cab, and went to the airport. On the flight home and for the next few weeks, I pondered the wonderful and dramatic time I'd had with Tom. It was difficult to say it was the end for me. I wasn't as emotionally invested as he. Although my feelings hadn't changed since we met, it seemed he wanted everything or nothing. We had different perspectives on our relationship due to our different stages of life. I had the possibility of sixty more years of life ahead of me. Tom maybe had ten. I saw a long road of experiences and mysteries, without the fear of impending death. As Tom said over and over, he was going to die soon. I didn't understand desperation then. I feared I had broken his heart. I would give it time and try again to make contact. I couldn't abandon him, not after what we shared, not after what I came to understand about his life. For now, I would let it go. I had a career to build, and that would take all my time and energy.

CHAPTER 10

YOURS TRULY, BLANCHE

CHICAGO: THE CORPORATE LIFE

As BlueCross BlueShield Association Manager of Consulting Services, I had my own office. It was a perfect eight-by-eight square full of unnecessary office equipment: a Selectric typewriter, multiline telephone, conferencing speakerphone, dry-erase board, corkboard, flipchart, two file cabinets, two chairs, and a large desk. It felt like a storage room.

Four people reported to me. One was a middle-aged man who always gave his point of view on things that were none of his concern. He loved to tell me how much he hated Italian food. Another was an overweight older man who managed the department until I displaced him. One day, he haughtily told me that research indicated short people are less likely to be successful than other people. I am five foot four. The third was a bear of a man who was lazy and did his best to avoid me.

It pleased me to not interact with him, because he was also a liar.

Last, there was an attractive black woman who instantly became a friend but would later accuse me of racism and sexual harassment when I had to RIF (reduction in force) her due to downsizing. Her charges were later dismissed. I was cast in the role of insensitive patriarch. We were a perfectly dysfunctional family.

Later, I would hire two additional women who were business contacts that I knew and liked. They each hired two more people who reported to them. We became a larger dysfunctional family. The two women competed for the role of discontented wife, each wanting me to take care of her children (direct reports) first. The children avoided Daddy—me—and ran to their respective mothers whenever they felt I was treating them poorly or giving preferential treatment to the other mother's children.

The last member of the family was my boss, an Italian bully from Philadelphia who wanted to be a mobster but settled for a job as the executive director of personnel for a health care association. At first, I was his favorite son. Overtime, he abused, insulted, and threatened me. Eventually, I grew to hate all of them.

After eight years of dysfunctional relationships and endless sleepless nights, I fired two members of the family. The remaining members' contempt for me grew. By my ninth year, frustrated and disgusted with the corporate world, I walked off the job. I was forty-one years old. My choice to build a career in the corporate world was disappointing, but I had learned a lot about business. I had essentially earned an MBA without going to business school.

After several months of unemployment, during which I helped another best friend die from HIV infection, I started my own consulting practice. At last, I found success and peace of mind, working as an independent consultant. I worked hard to build a reputation for doing good work. I convinced myself that consulting was like directing. Consultants coach people in how to perform their job; directors coach actors in how to perform their role. I had designed a life that made me reasonably happy.

In February 1983, a few months after last visiting Tom in Key West, I got a call at work from my friend Donna.

"Did you hear about Tennessee Williams?"

"No, what?" I had written Tom a letter a couple of months after my visit to Key West but didn't receive one in return.

"He died last night."

I instantly felt I was buried in cement. Things did not end well when I was last in Key West. He felt rejected by my not going to Australia with him. In spite of our differences, I assumed I would see him again. I felt guilty as if I was somewhat responsible for his death. If I were with him perhaps, this wouldn't have happened. I glanced at a calendar. He died almost a year to the day from when we first met: February 1982 to February 1983. I experienced the last year of Tennessee Williams's life in the role of "object of desire." I was with him for the significant events of his life in that last year. The loss weighed heavily on my mind.

I thought back to that first night at his home when he was overcome with fear and loneliness. I was perplexed when he would sob and murmur. I thought he was merely sad and being somewhat dramatic. Countless times, he would say, "I don't have much time. I don't want to die alone." I didn't understand what years of loss and desperation could do to a life. Now, as an older man, I have come to believe he was tormented by grief and despair, mourning the loss of everything he loved, profoundly lonely from fear of dying alone, never feeling truly loved. I represented a flicker of hope for a new life in Australia with a young, loving companion. But it could not be.

"What did he die from?" I asked.

"He choked on something." Donna was the most naturally funny person I knew. Even though she was telling me about the death of someone I cared about, it sounded as if she were telling a joke. Her delivery neutralized my emotion.

"Thank you for letting me know." I left my office in search of a newspaper. The *New York Times* had a long article that indicated Tom was found dead on the floor of his bedroom at the Hotel Elysee. He had choked on a bottle cap.

I flashed back to that night at the Hotel Elysee when he

was having a conversation with Eugene O'Neill while walking in his sleep. I remembered watching him rip open a Visine bottle with his teeth. With the cap in his mouth, he tossed his head back to squeeze a few drops into his eyes. With the cap still secure in his teeth, he screwed the bottle back into the cap and placed it on the side table. Unfortunately, he wasn't so agile the night he choked.

I imagined how that fateful night played itself out. He probably drank throughout the day, taking his multitude of pills with gulps of white wine. After stumbling to bed, he reached for the Visine bottle to relieve the pain in his tired, bloodshot eyes, unscrewed the bottle cap with his teeth, and tossed his head back to squeeze the refreshing drops into his eyes. This time, he sucked the cap down, and it lodged in his throat, blocking his breathing tube. He was too incapacitated to cough it up, his hands swollen with arthritis, unable to remove the plastic cap from his throat, and with no one there to administer the Heimlich maneuver, he asphyxiated and died. Could I have prevented it if I had been there? I ruminated about that for weeks.

The only person I knew how to contact was his friend John, Sebastian's lover. The conversation was brief. John told me the funeral would be held in St. Louis, and I should go there to pay my respects. He also told me that Tom talked about me quite a bit and that he liked me very much. I appreciated his telling me that, but it made me feel worse. I thanked him for the information.

I didn't like funerals and hadn't gone to one in years. I had come to believe funerals were an unnecessary ritual. Celebrating a life, rather than mourning it, was better. Going to his funeral would be meaningless to me. Instead, I went home and reread the journal of the amazing year I spent with Tennessee Williams, which is the basis for this book.

I also planned a pilgrimage to Key West to honor my literary hero. I wanted to revisit the places I had been with the man who was so kind to me. Being there would allow me to relive those sacred moments. It would be far better than a funeral. Within two weeks, I was back in Key West.

Albert graciously let me stay at his home. This time I would have my own bedroom. I was going to Key West alone to honor Tom and seal my memories of our time together. Albert was at work when I arrived, but his roommate, a lean young black man with painted fingernails and hair worn up in an oversized French twist, was there to let me in. With unbridled flirtatiousness, he flamboyantly welcomed me to Key West and Albert's home by wrapping his arms around me and giving me a wet kiss. I knew I had arrived. After showing me to my room, I unpacked and headed to Duval Street to rent a bike.

It was a piercing bright white-blue day. I leisurely retraced the route from the Monster that night we'd stopped for champagne and Scope on our way to Tom's house. As I approached his home, I could see it was uninhabited. Scaling the same fence I had on those nights Helen locked me out, I saw the pool area was arranged just like the night we first met. Lounge chairs were strewn about, with tattered low-hanging Chinese lanterns, extinguished long ago. The palm tree where we recited Shakespeare seemed smaller. An accumulation of dust made everything look as if it were covered in a gray tarp.

I peered through the sliding glass doors. The interior of the house was frozen in the same squalid way it was that last morning in September, when I left without saying good-bye. The same old crumpled furniture was laden with books and newspapers tossed about. His imprint was there, but it was lifeless. I sat on the porch where the cockatoo squawked that night we played in Violet Venable's garden.

Like an old silent movie, that first evening began to play in my mind, in Charlie Chaplin speed. The sailor, the con man, the ingénue, and the adoring fan were animated in sepia tones. The faded and flickering comedy/tragedy appeared like decaying celluloid in my mind. His tear-soaked face, contorted with misery, loomed in front of me, half tragic hero and half melting clown.

"*I don't want to die alone,*" he gasped as his frightened eyes searched my face for refuge. Sadly, he had died alone. As he lay choking on a bottle cap, no one was there to rescue him from the terror. What were his last thoughts? What words did he try to utter?

Love eluded him throughout his life. The stories he told about the people he loved were tragic.

"Frankie never said he loved me."

"My mother was a monster."

"I have known nothing but con men since Frankie died."

Those he loved most didn't love him in return, or at least never expressed it. I had let him down too. I never heard a story about a mutually loving relationship. I wondered if he ever felt loved. In spite of all that, a great playwright grew from the heart of a lonely, frightened genius who turned misery into poetry. His intense fear of dying alone must have meant that in the end he would have to face the terrifying truth. He died never feeling loved.

I wiped the tears from my eyes with the sweat-soaked T-shirt I was wearing. Where would I be right now if I had gone to Australia? Would he be alive? Would I be happier? After about an hour, I rode back to Albert's house. He graciously made me dinner and let me mourn Tom's passing a bit.

After dinner, I decided to go to the Monster alone, before the crowd arrived. I wanted the memory of him to fill the empty space, allowing me to walk unencumbered through the past as I reflected on our time together. It was twilight when I arrived. Like the aura of a dream, cobalt light shrouded the silent bar. The place was empty. At a distance, clanking bottles told me the bartender was setting up for the night. In the center of the dance floor, a canopy was set up, with a TV on a stage at the far end. Folding chairs were arranged as if it were a theater. I asked the bartender what was going on tonight.

Without interrupting his work, he said, "There is a special showing of Tennessee Williams's *A Streetcar Named Desire*." He was more intent on setting up the bar than on talking to me.

"With Ann Margret?" I asked.

"I think so. She seems all wrong for the part."

I didn't tell him that Tom thought differently. "May I have a white wine? I had to toast Tom with the drink we so often shared.

"Sure, no problem," the busy bartender answered. I walked under the canopy and sat in the back row of the makeshift theater.

Suddenly, unannounced, the teleplay began. No one set the stage, no memorial speech, no audience ... just me. The evening mysteriously came together, like the events we shared in his life. Tonight, I was swept up into the magic of his charmed and tragic life.

The production was three hours long. Ann Margret was the Blanche that Tom intended: vulnerable, sensual, truthful, tragic—to him, the quintessential qualities of life.

Serendipity brought me to the stairs of the Monster that first night; now it brought me back to the beginning of our time together to hear his eulogy in his own words, *A Streetcar Named Desire.*

In that last year of his life, he had become Blanche, after the doctor took her away from Stella and Stanley's apartment. He was Blanche, after surviving the sanitarium. Like Blanche, he was alone and frightened, abandoned and unloved. The bartender never looked at the TV. The entire event seemed arranged for me.

It was 9:00, and the dance crowd had begun to arrive. As I walked back to Albert's, I reflected on his eulogy ... the message inside the play. Through the character of Blanche, Tom dramatized his view of life.

We are fragile, sensual creatures ... alone ... life is full of enduring loss ... people can be cruel ... to love and be loved is the only refuge ... I have always depended on the kindness of strangers ...

An artist dies alone, drained of emotion, exhausted from filtering a dishonest world in search of sustainable truth. Tom embraced his passion and sacrificed himself to what he loved most—his art. He was driven to sit at his typewriter every day and render truth from life. He was the menagerie of characters he created. Collectively, they tell the story of what it means to be human. They are him.

The filmmaker in me died as well that night. Maybe Tom showed me I wasn't tortured enough to be an artist. I was no longer frustrated by the dilemma: art versus business. I would merge them. In time, I would transform my passion for film into a different voice as an independent, creative business consultant.

I left Key West two days later, feeling the pilgrimage sealed his place as a great mentor in my life. Each time I see his plays performed, I am reminded of him. All those personas are part of him.

In that last year of life, Tom opened his soul to me. I learned compassion. I saw the fear and pain of growing old, of dying alone, unloved, of seeing life fade into oblivion one piece at a time. This was not a character in one of his plays. This was Tennessee Williams.

His life and work are a testament to telling the truth about being human. We are born alone. We live alone. We die alone. Finding love is a journey laden with land mines, but being human means surviving in spite of the pain, the disappointment, and the despair—and perhaps that pain can be translated into something beautiful to help others learn and grow.

Although I saw his frightened heart, I never saw him doubt what he was doing. It took a great deal of courage for him to expose his vulnerability to an insensitive world. It took bravery to continue to write after he lost his voice. Our time together briefly distracted him from his fear. There was joy. There was sorrow. There was hope. Yes, he reached for a kind stranger to rescue him from falling down the stairs the night we met, but I couldn't rescue him from his frightened heart.

EPILOGUE

LIFE AND DEATH IN THE 1980S

CHICAGO: MY FRIGHTENED HEART

About three months after Tom's death, an article appeared in *New York* magazine about Tennessee Williams's last year. The writer stated that a "Sicilian from Chicago" taunted him in that last year. Toward the end of the article, Helen was asked about his last days. She was quoted saying, "The Sicilian called him an old man. He was never the same afterwards." Her vindictive words hurt me. I was never cruel to him. It was then I knew I would one day write this book to put the record straight.

Tom's bizarre death from choking on a bottle cap heralded a decade of many deaths for me. Like the gypsy in *Streetcar— los muertos, los muertos*—it was an omen of bad things to come. My best friend from college, Bob, was institutionalized after suffering a nervous breakdown. Before there were psychotropic drugs that lift depression, he had a series of life catastrophes that overwhelmed him. He was incapacitated for almost a year. It was as if my brother died.

The rest of my "gay family" contracted and died of AIDS between 1983 and 1994. Jon Cockrell, John Kauppilla, Carey South, Ronnie Pechler, Albert Osterman, Tunis Denise, and Rick Menke were my inner circle of friends. In all, I watched eighteen people die. They were all in their thirties.

We were at the age when men's emotional testicles drop, driven by how we feel instead of how we think. Sexual conquest was no longer the measure of a man. Careers were falling into place. Life's secrets were revealed. Lifetime bonds were sealed. Just when we took possession of our lives, they all died—and I was left alone.

I helped four of them die. Two of them asked me to be executor of their wills. It was painful to butcher their lives into parcels to be distributed to friends and family. This overwhelming number of deaths made me fear that anyone I would get close to would die. Tom's despair took root in me and began to grow.

I became celibate. Unsafe sex was rampant. People didn't know or divulge their HIV status in those days, out of fear of being ostracized. The HIV cocktail, which is a combination of medications specifically designed to combat the myriad forms of the virus, was not invented yet. Eventually, by the mid-1990s, the cocktail would allow those who were infected to live longer lives.

I stopped going to bars, socialized less, didn't answer my phone, and stopped reading newspapers. The news was filled with more and more deaths every day. A few people started making an AIDS-deaths quilt that traveled the country. The panels were designed and fabricated by friends and family and were meant to commemorate the life of a loved one. Sections were added, until it was too large to travel or be displayed. I felt smothered by the "quilt" because I survived when so many died, I isolated myself from the world.

At first, I embraced my aloneness. Being alone is a choice; being lonely is fear. I rationalized that being alone was the natural state of the human experience. Learning to feel good alone is learning how to love oneself. Lonely was sad. Alone was learning through reflection and growth. Lonely was isolating. Alone was enriching. That mind-set was brief. Eventually, the onslaught of so many deaths overwhelmed me, and I became very depressed, alone, and lonely.

My last long term, intimate relationship ended when I was in my late thirties. I never pursued another one. It's been almost thirty years now that I have been single. As more and more people got sick and died, I began to frequently cry for no apparent reason, like Tom. My life became a void. Tom's swollen, tear-filled face would often loom in my mind. I began to better understand his frequently spontaneous sorrowful outbursts of tears.

Jon Cockrell and Ron Pechler died of pneumonia.

John Kauppilla died of toxoplasmosis.

Carey South died of Kaposi sarcoma.

Tunis Denise and Rick Menke died of a combination of virulent diseases.

It was the mid-1990s. The deaths of all my beautiful, young, and talented friends were like experiencing a mother's death every year for ten years. I was emotionally frozen. Like Tom, I recoiled from affection. Closeness would make me vulnerable. I was in my early forties at that time. I felt my life was coming to an end. Tom had said over and over again, *I'm dying, I'm dying, I'm dying.* I now understood where that came from. Every loss made him feel he was dying, a bit at a time.

When Tom and I first met, I was thirty-four; he was seventy-one. I hadn't experienced enough of life to understand why he was so sad. I didn't know then how confining life could be. Compassion opens up a lens on living a good, loving life, but it also increases vulnerability—I learned that from Tom. After so many deaths, I learned how loss leaves emptiness, and how emptiness leads to despair and fear.

In that last year of his life, Tom was no longer able to dissect the human heart with the poetic precision that defined his genius. Everything and everyone he loved were gone. Every day was a struggle to avoid loneliness, to elude despair. A lifetime of success didn't insulate his heart from fear; only the numbness that comes from alcohol and drugs made life tolerable. Although his recent work was no longer revered, he courageously continued to write. He was never afraid to tap his soul for truth, never afraid to hold up a mirror to reveal hypocrisy, never afraid to expose his vulnerability.

Scratching for love like Maggie the Cat, like Blanche, desperately longing for kindness as a remedy for cruelty, like Lady, hoping for a new beginning, he triumphed over death. Sadly, his greatest fear came true. He died alone. However, I'd like to think he wasn't alone that night. Instead, while gasping for air, his menagerie of characters was with him, reminding him of how much life he lived and understood. Like the night at the Goodman Theatre, when he coached the characters to come to life, so too he was talking to them as he faded into oblivion. He was them. His death sealed their immortality and his.

I keep the silver heart the Goodman gave him in an ornate silver box on a dresser near my bed. It's blackened with tarnish now. I remember the night he threw it to the floor in disgust. "Worthless!" he'd painfully cried.

I'd lifted it up as if it were a sacred relic. It was new and shiny then. I witnessed another loss that night; it was the end of his love affair with the theater.

I look at the tarnished heart from time to time and remember the kind poet who exposed his frightened heart to me, who taught me what it means to be human and showed me what can happen when we grow old, alone and unloved. It was the year I redefined my life, from hopeful artist to successful independent consultant, from boy to man.

Now in my sixties, I have come to realize that a creative spirit can be expressed in many different ways. For twenty-five years, I have had a successful consulting business—coaching executives, managers, and salespeople in how to communicate effectively in their respective roles. Communication is our lifeline to connecting with others. It's an art. Most people are very poor at it.

Artists like Tom are the greatest communicators, transmitters of what it means to be human, their art a blueprint for life. It tells us who we are, shows us how to live a good life, and enables us to understand how to feel joy and sorrow. Being a conscious human being, striving for happiness, learning how to love, and earning the love of others are the things that ultimately define who we are. These are the things that measure a life; these are the truths art communicates. Universal, profound art continues communicating long after the artist dies.

My heart is no longer frightened. I have learned to embrace life. It's all we have. With humility and courage, I strive to understand its vicissitudes and injustices, accepting the inevitable, letting it go. Each time I see a Tennessee Williams play, he is communicating what it means to be human. I hear him speaking those words. Perhaps immortality is what attracted me most to being an artist. Contributing something meaningful to life, helping others to learn and grow is the greatest gift we can have and the greatest gift we can leave behind. It is immortality.

Printed in the United States
By Bookmasters